First World War
and Army of Occupation
War Diary
France, Belgium and Germany

32 DIVISION
97 Infantry Brigade
Highland Light Infantry
17th (Service) Battalion (3rd Glasgow)
21 November 1915 - 31 January 1918

WO95/2403/3

The Naval & Military Press Ltd
www.nmarchive.com
Published in association with The National Archives

Published by

The Naval & Military Press Ltd

Unit 10 Ridgewood Industrial Park,

Uckfield, East Sussex,

TN22 5QE England

Tel: +44 (0) 1825 749494

www.naval-military-press.com

www.nmarchive.com

This diary has been reprinted in facsimile from the original. Any imperfections are inevitably reproduced and the quality may fall short of modern type and cartographic standards.

© Crown Copyright
Images reproduced by permission of The National Archives, London, England, 2015.

Contents

Document type	Place/Title	Date From	Date To
Heading	WO95/2403-3 97 Inf Bde 17 Btn HLI Nov 1915-Jan 19		
Heading	32nd Division 97th Infy Bde 17th. Bn High'D Lt Infy Nov 1915-Jan 1918 Disbanded		
Heading	32nd Division 17th H.L.I. Vol I Nov 15		
War Diary	Codford Wiltshire	21/11/1915	21/11/1915
War Diary	Le Havre	22/11/1915	23/11/1915
War Diary	Mouflers	24/11/1915	26/11/1915
War Diary	La Chaussee	27/11/1915	27/11/1915
War Diary	Molliens-Au-Bois	28/11/1915	30/11/1915
Heading	32nd Div 19th H.L.I. Vol. 2 1915		
War Diary	Bouzincourt	01/12/1915	07/12/1915
War Diary	Trenches Sub Sector F.1.	08/12/1915	11/12/1915
War Diary	Molliens-Au-Bois	12/12/1915	21/12/1915
War Diary	Bouzincourt	22/12/1915	22/12/1915
War Diary	Trenches Sub. Sect F.1.	23/12/1915	26/12/1915
War Diary	Bouzincourt	27/12/1915	30/12/1915
War Diary	Trenches Sub-Sect F.1	31/12/1915	31/12/1915
Heading	17th HLI. Vol. 3 Tail		
War Diary	Trenches Sub-Sector F.1.	01/01/1916	06/01/1916
War Diary	Aveluy	07/01/1916	13/01/1916
War Diary	Trenches Sub Sector F.1.	14/01/1916	20/01/1916
War Diary	Bouzincourt	21/01/1916	27/01/1916
War Diary	Trenches F.1.	28/01/1916	31/01/1916
Heading	97th Brigade 32nd Division. 17th Battalion Highland Light Infantry February 1916		
Heading	War Diary of 17th Bn. H.L.I. From 1st February 1916 to 29th February 1916 (Volume I)		
Miscellaneous			
War Diary	Trenches F.1.	01/02/1916	04/02/1916
War Diary	Aveluy	05/02/1916	10/02/1916
War Diary	Trenches F.1.	11/02/1916	16/02/1916
War Diary	Millencourt	17/02/1916	23/02/1916
War Diary	Nenencourt	24/02/1916	28/02/1916
War Diary	Dernancourt	29/02/1916	29/02/1916
Map	Report War Diary 17th H.L.I. Appendix I		
Heading	97th Brigade. 32nd Division. 17th Battalion Highland Light Infantry March 1916		
War Diary	Dernancourt	01/03/1916	09/03/1916
War Diary	Trenches E.1	10/03/1916	16/03/1916
War Diary	Albert	17/03/1916	22/03/1916
War Diary	Trenches E.1.	23/03/1916	28/03/1916
War Diary	Dernancourt	29/03/1916	31/03/1916
Heading	War Diary of 17th (S) B.H.L.I. Month of March 1916		
War Diary	Dernancourt	01/04/1916	03/04/1916
War Diary	Bouzincourt	04/04/1916	11/04/1916
War Diary	Trenches Authville Sub. Sector.	12/04/1916	16/04/1916
War Diary	Aveluy	17/04/1916	20/04/1916
War Diary	Trenches. Authville Sub. Sector.	21/04/1916	23/04/1916
War Diary	Bouzincourt	24/04/1916	30/04/1916
Heading	War Diary of 17th (S) B.H.L.I. April 1916		

Heading	97th Brigade. 32nd Division. 17th Battalion Highland Light Infantry May 1916		
War Diary	Bouzincourt	01/05/1916	04/05/1916
War Diary	Rubempre	05/05/1916	16/05/1916
War Diary	Warloy	17/05/1916	17/05/1916
War Diary	Aveluy	18/05/1916	21/05/1916
War Diary	Trenches Authville Sub. Sector	22/05/1916	25/05/1916
War Diary	Crucifix Corner	26/05/1916	30/05/1916
War Diary	Warloy	31/05/1916	31/05/1916
Heading	97th Brigade. 32nd Division. 1/17th Battalion Highland Light Infantry June 1916		
War Diary	Warloy	01/06/1916	11/06/1916
War Diary	Contay	12/06/1916	22/06/1916
War Diary	Warloy	23/06/1916	23/06/1916
War Diary	Senlis	24/06/1916	26/06/1916
War Diary	Bouzincourt	27/06/1916	30/06/1916
Heading	War Diary of 17th (S) Battn HLI From 1st July, 1916 to 31st July 1916 Vol 9		
War Diary	Trenches British and German	01/07/1916	01/07/1916
War Diary	British Trenches	02/07/1916	02/07/1916
War Diary	Coucrfex Corner	03/07/1916	03/07/1916
War Diary	Contay	04/07/1916	07/07/1916
War Diary	Senlis	08/07/1917	08/07/1917
War Diary	British Trenches	09/07/1916	15/07/1916
War Diary	Ampliers	16/07/1916	16/07/1916
War Diary	Sus St Leger	17/07/1916	18/07/1916
War Diary	Ternas	19/07/1916	19/07/1916
War Diary	Tangry	20/07/1916	20/07/1916
War Diary	Allonagne	21/07/1916	25/07/1916
War Diary	Allonagne-Bethune	26/07/1916	26/07/1916
War Diary	Bethune	27/07/1916	31/07/1916
Heading	War Diary of 17th (S) Bn. H.L.I. From 1st July 1916 to 31st July 1916		
Heading	War Diary of 17th (S) Bn. Highland Light Infantry From 1st August 1916 to 31st Aug. 1916 Volume 1		
War Diary	Bethune	01/08/1916	05/08/1916
War Diary	Trenches. (Cambrin Sub. Sector)	06/08/1916	10/08/1916
War Diary	Annequin	11/08/1916	14/08/1916
War Diary	Trenches	15/08/1916	21/08/1916
War Diary	Beuvry	22/08/1916	23/08/1916
War Diary	Mazingarbe	24/08/1916	24/08/1916
War Diary	Trenches	25/08/1916	28/08/1916
War Diary	Philosophe	29/08/1916	31/08/1916
Heading	War Diary. 17th. Batt H L I From 1st Sept. 1916 till 30th Sept. 1916 Volume XI		
War Diary	Annezin	01/09/1916	08/09/1916
War Diary	Cuinchy (Left Sub Sector)	09/09/1916	12/09/1916
War Diary	Cuinchy	13/09/1916	15/09/1916
War Diary	Left Sub Sector	16/09/1916	17/09/1916
War Diary	Cuinchy (Left. Sub Sector)	18/09/1916	25/09/1916
War Diary	Bethune.	26/09/1916	30/09/1916
Heading	War Diary (from 1st Oct 1916 to 31st Oct. 1916) Vol III		
War Diary	Bethune	01/10/1916	03/10/1916
War Diary	Trenches (Maison Rouge) Cambrin Right Sub Sector	04/10/1916	07/10/1916
War Diary	Trenches (Maison Rouge) Cambrin Right Section	08/10/1916	08/10/1916
War Diary	Trenches	09/10/1916	11/10/1916

War Diary	Trenches Cambrin Right Sub Section	12/10/1916	14/10/1916
War Diary	Beuvry	15/10/1916	15/10/1916
War Diary	Labeuvriere	16/10/1916	16/10/1916
War Diary	Su Thieuloye	17/10/1916	17/10/1916
War Diary	Monts En Ternois	18/10/1916	18/10/1916
War Diary	Hardinval	19/10/1916	21/10/1916
War Diary	Rubempre	22/10/1916	23/10/1916
War Diary	Bouzincourt	24/10/1916	30/10/1916
War Diary	Rubempre	31/10/1916	31/10/1916
Heading	War Diary 1st to 30th November, 1916 (inclusive) Volume 12		
War Diary	Val-De-Maison	01/11/1916	13/11/1916
War Diary	Vadencourt	14/11/1916	14/11/1916
War Diary	Martinsart Valley	15/11/1916	15/11/1916
War Diary	Englebelmer	16/11/1916	17/11/1916
War Diary	Beaumont. Hamel	17/11/1916	19/11/1916
War Diary	Mailly-Maillet.	20/11/1916	23/11/1916
War Diary	Raincheval	24/11/1916	25/11/1916
War Diary	Beauval	26/11/1916	26/11/1916
War Diary	Franqueville	27/11/1916	30/11/1916
Heading	17th Service. Battalion Highland Light Infantry War Diary. 1st December 1916-31st Dec 1916 Vol 14		
War Diary	Franqueville.	01/12/1916	16/12/1916
War Diary	Bertaucourt.	17/12/1916	17/12/1916
War Diary	Rubempre	18/12/1916	05/01/1917
War Diary	Courcelles	06/01/1917	06/01/1917
War Diary	Trenches	07/01/1917	10/01/1917
War Diary	Courcelles	11/01/1917	12/01/1917
War Diary	Trenches	13/01/1917	15/01/1917
War Diary	Bus.	16/01/1917	20/01/1917
War Diary	Trenches	21/01/1917	31/01/1917
Heading	War Diary. From 1st February to 28th February 1917 Volume V		
War Diary	Lyntham Camp	01/02/1917	02/02/1917
War Diary	Trenches	03/02/1917	13/02/1917
War Diary	Mailly Maillet	14/02/1917	14/02/1917
War Diary	Bolton Camp	15/02/1917	17/02/1917
War Diary	Molliens-Au-Bois	18/02/1917	21/02/1917
War Diary	Camon	22/02/1917	22/02/1917
War Diary	Wiencourt	23/02/1917	25/02/1917
War Diary	Le. Quesnel	26/02/1917	28/02/1917
Heading	War Diary From 1st March To 31st March 1917 Volume No VI		
War Diary	Le Quesnel	01/03/1917	02/03/1917
War Diary	Ney Post	03/03/1917	05/03/1917
War Diary	Kuropatkin	06/03/1917	08/03/1917
War Diary	Ney Post	09/03/1917	12/03/1917
War Diary	Kuropatkin	13/03/1917	14/03/1917
War Diary	Le Quesnel	15/03/1917	17/03/1917
War Diary	Bouchon	18/03/1917	18/03/1917
War Diary	Fresnoy	19/03/1917	19/03/1917
War Diary	Nesle	20/03/1917	28/03/1917
War Diary	Germaine	29/03/1917	31/03/1917
Heading	17th H.L.I. War Diary From 1st To 30th April 1917 Vol No. 6		
War Diary	Germaine & Savy	01/04/1917	01/04/1917

War Diary	Savy	01/04/1917	01/04/1917
War Diary	Fluquieres-Douchy Rd.	02/04/1917	05/04/1917
War Diary	Germaine & Francilly Selency	06/04/1917	06/04/1917
War Diary	Francilly Selency	07/04/1917	09/04/1917
War Diary	Francilly Selency & Holnon	10/04/1917	10/04/1917
War Diary	Holnon	11/04/1917	13/04/1917
War Diary	Holnon Fayet	14/04/1917	15/04/1917
War Diary	Germaine	16/04/1917	18/04/1917
War Diary	Germaine Canizy	19/04/1917	19/04/1917
War Diary	Canizy	19/04/1917	30/04/1917
Heading	17th (S) Batt. Highland L.I. War Diary 1st. May To 31st. May 1917. No 7. Vol 19		
War Diary	Canizy	01/05/1917	14/05/1917
War Diary	Canizy Voyennes Nesle Curchy	15/05/1917	15/05/1917
War Diary	Curchy Rosieres	16/05/1917	16/05/1917
War Diary	Rosieres Hangard	17/05/1917	17/05/1917
War Diary	Hangard	18/05/1917	29/05/1917
War Diary	Hangard Villers-Bretonneux	30/05/1917	30/05/1917
War Diary	Villers-Bretonneux	31/05/1917	31/05/1917
Heading	17th S.B. H.L.I. War Diary 1st-30th June 1917 Vol 20		
War Diary	Villers-Brettonneux	01/06/1917	02/06/1917
War Diary	Doulieu	03/06/1917	13/06/1917
War Diary	Doulieu Eecke	14/06/1917	14/06/1917
War Diary	Eecke	15/06/1917	15/06/1917
War Diary	Eecke Mardyck	16/06/1917	16/06/1917
War Diary	Mardyck	17/06/1917	17/06/1917
War Diary	Mardyck Petite-Synthe	18/06/1917	18/06/1917
War Diary	Petite-Synthe Coxyde	19/08/1917	19/08/1917
War Diary	Coxyde & Camp Kuhn	20/06/1917	20/06/1917
War Diary	Oost Dunkerke (Camp Kuhn)	21/06/1917	24/06/1917
War Diary	Oost Dunkerke & Nieuport (Petit Redan)	25/06/1917	25/06/1917
War Diary	Nieuport (Petit Redan)	26/06/1917	29/06/1917
War Diary	Nieuport (New Parade)	30/06/1917	30/06/1917
Heading	War Diary. From 1st July to 31st July 1917 Volume 9		
War Diary		01/07/1917	31/07/1917
Heading	War Diary From 1st August 1917 To 31st August 1917 Volume No. 10		
War Diary		01/08/1917	31/08/1917
Heading	War Diary From September 1 To September 30 1917 Volume No 11 17 HLI Vol 23		
War Diary		01/09/1917	30/09/1917
Heading	Volume 12 Lt. Colonel Commanding 17th (S) Bn. H.L.I.		
War Diary		01/10/1917	31/10/1917
Heading	War Diary From Nov. 1. 1917 Till Nov. 30. 1917 Vol. No. 13 17 HLI Vol 25		
War Diary		01/11/1917	30/11/1917
Heading	War Diary From. December 1, 1917 To 31, 1917 Vol 11 17 HLI Vol 26		
War Diary		01/12/1917	31/12/1917
Heading	War Diary From January 1, 1918 To January 31, 1918 Volume 12.		
War Diary		01/01/1918	31/01/1918

WO 95/2403/3
97 INF BDE
17 Bn HLI Nov 1915 - Jan 1918

32ND DIVISION
97TH INFY BDE

17TH BN HIGH'D LT INFY

NOV 1915 - JAN 1918

DISBANDED

33 mT Zwecin

17th Atzl.
tot I

121/7693

Nov 15

WAR DIARY

INTELLIGENCE SUMMARY

(Erase heading not required.)

Army Form C. 2118

Instructions regarding War Diaries and Intelligence Summaries are contained in F.S. Regs., Part II. and the Staff Manual respectively. Title Pages will be prepared in manuscript.

Place	Date	Hour	Summary of Events and Information	Remarks and references to Appendices
Codford Wiltshire	21st Nov.	10 a.m.	Medical + unit inspection of arms, equipment. This inspection. Battalion strength 1032 including Commg Officer + ammunition.	
Le Havre	22nd / 23rd Nov.		Battalion left Codford by rail in two parties at 8 a.m. & 9.15 a.m. respectively for Southampton. Two transports conveyed the troops across the channel on calm sunny weather to Le Havre, the Battalion landing without a single thing on the another boat. At 7 a.m. on the 23rd the troops without transport left the docks & marched 3 miles to Rest Camp No.5 when the rest of the day was spent under canvas. Brief account of	France "Amiens"
Mouflers	24th / 25th Nov.		the Battalion (Hdq 250 men & 6 officers) left from Gare station Havre 3 at 1.15 p.m. rapid transpt 2 coys with them. Rations at rest Pavre. The remainder left from Pavre 4 at 2.30 p.m. and proceeded via Havre & early the morning. There was an average 25 men to which have been compelled although local transport from by Rouen & Amiens to Pont Remy when the troops arrived in early hours of 25th Nov. Leaving at 6.30 a.m. a march of 9 miles led them to Mouflers. On being served with rations. Arriving there about 10 a.m. billeting was soon completed at 4.30 p.m. Only the Maire, adjutant and three orderlies have been by the Billeting Officer. On billets for 150 men at the Jolie Auberge was unavailable thing in a firing order. A rather day with bright bugles atmosphere.	Rfce Map FRANCE "Amiens" Sheet 600

J.B.C. & A. A.D.S.S./Forms/C. 2118.

Army Form C. 2118

WAR DIARY
or
INTELLIGENCE SUMMARY
(Erase heading not required.)

Instructions regarding War Diaries and Intelligence Summaries are contained in F. S. Regs, Part II. and the Staff Manual respectively. Title Pages will be prepared in manuscript.

Place	Date	Hour	Summary of Events and Information	Remarks and references to Appendices
Mouflers	26th Nov.		The Battalion rested in Billets. A quiet fine day.	Refs. Map FRANCE "Amiens" 17/North 80,000
La Chaussée	27th Nov.		The Battalion left billets at 8.15 a.m. & moved to starting point "La Folie Auberge" at 8.30 a.m. Following an even slower rate 17/North Fres., 202nd Coy. A.S.C. and 205th Coy. A.S.C. marched through Flixecourt — Bellay-sur-Somme to La Chaussée (8 miles) arriving there at 11.30 a.m. and into billets. Billeting area spread 520 men & 180 officers in Château at Tirancourt. Keen frost — fine programme.	
Molliens-au-Bois	28th Nov.		The Battalion left billets at 8.15 a.m. & marched to starting point & moved at St. Sauveur at 9 a.m. when they were ready were held by other units passing before them same point of route over. After another — through rain — to Rainneville — Bertangles. From there the Battalion marched by way via Coisy and Rainneville to Molliens-au-Bois arriving in billets. Distance 11 miles. Keen frost — 1–15 but fair. Very two trucks were in difficulties & men fell out, but two men were missing. Bachamps joined the 13 Battalion was attached to A Coy. for rations.	
"	29th Nov.		The Battalion rested in billets. Some improvements were effected on the sanitary annex — cookhouse. A day of very heavy rain.	
"	30th Nov.		The day was spent — making clothes — men attending to feet. Rain unceasing throughout & weather frame.	

1875 W.t. W593/826 1,000,000 4/15 J.B.C. & A. A.D.S.S./Forms/C. 2118.

121/1936

Army Form C. 2118

Instructions regarding War Diaries and Intelligence Summaries are contained in F. S. Regs., Part II. and the Staff Manual respectively. Title Pages will be prepared in manuscript.

WAR DIARY
or
INTELLIGENCE SUMMARY
(Erase heading not required.)

3

Place	Date	Hour	Summary of Events and Information	Remarks and references to Appendices
Bouzincourt	1st Dec.		The Battalion left billets in Mollens at 8-15 a.m. marched followed by the 16th N.F. & to Beaucourt where a Company of the 17th North. Fus. joined the column. At Warloy two of our Coys (viz Left Wing Battalion) joined & went on the night to Millencourt where they have into billets (9½ miles) the right Wing Battalion continues on through Senlis to Bouzincourt & went into billets where (11½ miles.) Being attached for rations & supplies to Ch. 153rd Brigade the officers and N.C.Os of right Wing Battalion proceeded between 4 and 5 p.m. to Averluy & went into front line French Sub Sections F.1 and 2. occupied by the 1/7 Gordons and 1/7 Black Watch. Two missed aging.	Refer Map FRANCE "Albert" (continuous sheet) 1/40,000
—do—	2nd Dec.		The men of the right wing Battalion remained in their new billets working hard from the Left wing Battalion were engaged until evening on the bivouacs. Very cold day.	
—do—	3rd Dec.		The right-wing Battalion returned to billets. The bivouacs were in rather crowded after the two front companies arrived. A large force of French M.C.Os of the Left Wing Battalion from Millencourt, all the officers and 9 n.c.os were ordered. In accompany the 2nd Lieut officers proceeded to the above front line billets joined the 5th Gordons into (2nd our Coy.) & relieved 3 Coys of the 1/7 Gordons, and the 1/7 Black Watch. Again very cold. JMM M.F.	

1375 Wt. W593/326 1,000,000 4/15 J.B.C. & A. A.D.S.S./Forms/C. 2118.

WAR DIARY
or
INTELLIGENCE SUMMARY

Army Form C. 2118

Place	Date	Hour	Summary of Events and Information	Remarks and references to Appendices
Bezincourt	4th Dec		The men of the Regt. Eng. Battalion joined their officers & N.C.Os. in front line trenches. Some artillery action from 12:30 to 2:15 p.m. on both sides. Rumour shells fired in answer to Brig. Jl. Q. in Aveluy. A nice dry unit very little rain.	Ref. Map FRANCE "Albert" (outline sheet) 1/40,000
" "	5th Dec		Working parties from Regt. Eng. Battalion engaged in various Regt. Eng. Battalion entries to Millencourt. Nice unit little rain jam.	
" "	6th Dec		The four Companies relieved the Coys of 4" Royal Lancs. Reg. in F.1. and the Coys of 4" North Lan. Reg. in F.2. Slow fire on enemy trenches in afternoon from 6. Fire on enemy transport wagons. Rifle Grenades on 134/5 chimneys. Nice unit.	
" "	7th Dec		Conduct of trenches went on as usual. Rifle grenades used. Snipping parties to keep down m.g. work. Again rifle grenades in 134/5 r.m. & avenue. Dry mute.	
Tuesday Dec 8th 2nd Sector F.1.	8th Dec		Two Coys in F.2 moved into F.1. 7 N.O. of 8" Kings Regt (Liver) Liverpool moved into trenches. Lt Colonel Fagan to whom reported. Main operation at La Boisselle area 2h. Rifle Grenades & airways of own rifle. Rumour from Sector N. Coy.	
" "	9th Dec		Rumour O'McDowell A.Coy. wounded by a rifle Rumour Ins. Taylor & Cross, D. Coy. wounded by rifle fire. Scrimger on my any and enemy.	

J.M.M. J.H.O.
17 JH

WAR DIARY or INTELLIGENCE SUMMARY

Army Form C. 2118

(Erase heading not required.)

Instructions regarding War Diaries and Intelligence Summaries are contained in F.S. Regs., Part II. and the Staff Manual respectively. Title Pages will be prepared in manuscript.

Place	Date	Hour	Summary of Events and Information	Remarks and references to Appendices
Trenches Sec Sec C1 F1.	10th Dec		Very quiet all day; some M.G. fire at night. Very heavy rain fell at night.	
— do —	11th Dec		More dug outs excavated also M.G. emplacement. Many items of equipment lost. Trenches in very bad state. Battalion relieved in afternoon. Regt. having arrived. Passed R. McKelvie B Coy wounded slightly. Two Coys to Bourguignonne, 2 Coys to Millencourt. HQrs guard and Rest union.	
Millencourt and Bois	12th Dec		Battalion marched to Molliens arriving 3.30 p.m. Severe snow blizzard.	
	13th Dec		A day day until 4 p.m. Battalion marched up a Bouzique ay.	
	14th Dec		Battalion in training, working, cleaning. Wet and muddy.	
	15th Dec		— do — Inspected by C.O. Wet muddy	
	16th Dec		Inspected by G.O.C. Division. Wet muddy.	
	17th Dec		Battalion in training. Wet muddy	
	18th Dec		Route march of 8 miles. Dry sunny	
	19th Dec		Church Parade. Inspection of Companies by O.C. Bouzique ay.	
	20th Dec		Route march of 10 miles. Dry sunny	

WAR DIARY or INTELLIGENCE SUMMARY

Army Form C. 2118

(Erase heading not required.)

Instructions regarding War Diaries and Intelligence Summaries are contained in F.S. Regs., Part II. and the Staff Manual respectively. Title Pages will be prepared in manuscript.

Place	Date	Hour	Summary of Events and Information	Remarks and references to Appendices
Molliens au-Bois	21st Dec.	10am	Company inspections. Kit inspection.	
Bouzincourt	22nd Dec.		Battalion turned out 8 am. Marched via Baizieux and Hénencourt to Bouzincourt, arriving at 1.15 p.m. in heavy rain. Former province to bivouac when Battalion in places covered by 12 to 3" Serpentine only. Some very strong, and accordingly little use to the road.	
Tremonts Sub Sect F.1.	23rd Dec.		Moved into trenches in relief of... and relieved 11th Border Regiment. Very quiet on whole front. Strong main all day. Night came many casualties in the trenches. Continuous pumping required where commenced on. Woont S.W. Bouvincourt 28.8."	
— do —	24th Dec.		On our immediate during night near Crucifix Corner. Two very bad casualties on communication trench caused enemy shells in its traffic, there was a communication way in front of former line, where much of repair was necessary. Enemy was commenced near Crucifix Corner. Woont S.W. Bon 28.9	
— do —	25th Dec.		Strong Kaffir in old trench trench, two arrive in morning. The enemy churches have some artillery was active at 12 noon approx at 3pm in direction of Pozieres. Two have own some some cons of "Fevre Tree". Our Trench Mr. fired 250 rounds. Woont S.W. Bon 29.3	
— do —	26th Dec.		After his day rapid fix connents of the communication trenches were improves which were too shallow in Bouvinnet. Sap approach side are covered.	M.M.g.F.O. 17241.D.

1875—W. W.593/825 1,000,000 4/15 J.B.C. & A. A.D.S.S./Forms/C. 2118.

Army Form C. 2118

WAR DIARY
or
INTELLIGENCE SUMMARY
(Erase heading not required.)

Instructions regarding War Diaries and Intelligence Summaries are contained in F.S. Regs., Part II. and the Staff Manual respectively. Title Pages will be prepared in manuscript.

Place	Date	Hour	Summary of Events and Information	Remarks and references to Appendices
Trenches Sub-Sec. F.1.	26th Dec	(contd)	...averaged at 3 p.m. Enemy has been active with Whiz-bangs rifle grenades intermittently all day. Our artillery retaliated at noon. Wind S. Bar. 29.5".	
Bouzincourt	27th Dec		The Battalion was relieved in afternoon by 11th Borders Regiment, one man wounded near Crucifix Corner, arrived all quiet during relief. Marched to Bouzincourt and went into huts + tents for night. Day cold. Wind W.	
"	28th Dec		The Battalion moved into huts/tents Training by Companies. Beautiful day.	
"	29th Dec		The whole day spent in full inspections, supervisions, cleaning equipment	
"	30th Dec		— do —	
Trenches Sub-Sec F.1	31st Dec		The Battalion relieved the 11th Borders Regiment in Sub-Sect. F.1. relief was complete by 4.30. After a day's rest the men again free heavily. Wind S.E. Barom. 29.6"	

J.M. "14th" N.F.9.

17 de mayo
lot: 3

Army Form C. 2118

WAR DIARY
INTELLIGENCE SUMMARY
(Erase heading not required.)

Place	Date	Hour	Summary of Events and Information	Remarks and references to Appendices
Trenches Sub-section F.1.	1916 1st Jany.		This sub-sector F.1. lies east of Aveluy camp 2,000 yards and extends a frontage of 1,500 yards from X.7.3.6 X.13.a. inclusive. On our left in F.2 occupies by 1st & 4th his Battalions of 97" Brigade and on our right in E.3. occupies by 4th. 18" Division, in front of Albert. Enemy very any Gun active at 1 a.m. 2 a.m. and 11.15 p.m. A rifle comm. was Fed. ammun. lower Donnet where ememn. Coy is. That us damage done, two been civilies. By 9 pm. Wind S.E. Bar. 29.7 rising.	Refs. FRANCE 57. D S.E 1/20000
do	2nd Jany.		Thin am a talk alarm of g in on our right at 10.15 a.m. Gas exploded his mine at 3.15 p.m. at La Boisselle.	
do	3rd Jany.		Enemy shelled lower Donnet & Post Donnet intermittently all day. Capt. Houston of D. Coy. killed by a direct hit. his shelter was wire on our left from X.78.9.8 with Good effect.	
do	4th Jany.		Weather sitll dry wind W., Baron. 30.1." Enemy again shelled Donnets. Between 4 & 4.30 p.m. front entrance of Artillery, M.R. own right fire came 3 miles to north. — Beaumont-Hamel. Our Aeroplanes shelled trenches opposite 136 at 3.40 p.m. Line there did not fire.	
do	5th Jany.		Our Guns bombarded Ovillers and La Boisselle. Enemy's on Post Donnet. Our men recovery ammunent. Again heavy firing heard to north. Hostile aeroplane forces to retire by anti. aircraft guns at 10.30 a.m. M.M.K.J. 17.	

1875   Wt. W.593/826   1,000,000   4/15   J.B.C. & A.   A.D.S.S./Forms/C. 2118.

Army Form C. 2118

WAR DIARY
INTELLIGENCE SUMMARY
(Erase heading not required.)

Place	Date	Hour	Summary of Events and Information	Remarks and references to Appendices
Trenches Sussex F.1.	6" Jany.		As usual 20 shells into enemy front line trench to our left front in support O.P. Enemy retaliation on our front line 13S, damaged parapet. Very quiet all day. New fire steps are being made to front line and work all over gun on cable. Weir W. Baron 29.7	
Aveluy	7" Jany.		9th Battalion arrived today at 12.30 p.m. by Ch 11th Border Regiment. Proceeded to Trenches in Aveluy. Scouts billeting by Companies.	
— do —	8" Jany.		Cleaning equipment and trenching. One Coy trenching, three coys on fatigues, on working parties.	
— do —	9" Jany.		As above. Coy. officers inspect depures of village.	
— do —	10" Jany.		As above. Owing to demand for working parties it is almost impossible to have any parade or inspections but Coys have interior economy at villa.	
— do —	11" Jany.		As above. Privt: Adams of D Coy. killed by shell fire near Lower Donnel.	
— do —	12" Jany.		As above. Bombing practise and demonstrations. Lieut. Coy. Fortune wounded. — C Coy 3 men. B Coy 1 Sore.	
— do —	13" Jany.		As above. Throughout the week in trenches weather has been very mild and very showery.	

J.W.L.17.3.29.

Army Form C. 2118

10.

WAR DIARY
INTELLIGENCE SUMMARY
(Erase heading not required.)

Instructions regarding War Diaries and Intelligence Summaries are contained in F.S. Regs., Part II. and the Staff Manual respectively. Title Pages will be prepared in manuscript.

Place	Date	Hour	Summary of Events and Information	Remarks and references to Appendices
Trenches Sub-sector F.1.	14 Jany 1916.		The Battalion relieved the 11th Border Reg. today, relief being completed by 11-30 a.m. An enemy bombarded La Boisselle and Pozières during the afternoon. A British aeroplane was hummed thoroughly down behind E.3 (?) when it appeared to take fire. No one injured. Aplin observation Balloon was up and taken notes. A bright dry day.	
" " "	15 Jany.		During the day the enemy seemed intermittent artillery fire. Six work on the trenches goes on unchecked, and our own work about equally on the trenches. Lower W.	
" " "	16 Jany.		Enemy fired 14 shells into Lower Donnet. Our mine exploded La Boisselle was twice bombarded in afternoon. Enemy retaliated with 12 shells on our right sector, killing one man & wounding 2. Patrols were sent in early morning and early evening against enemy in front of our right sector with a view to cutting a new trench to cut off the entrance. Lower S.W. sap. see map. Bm. 29.9."	
" " "	17 Jany.		Artillery on both sides active today, our own concentrated 26 aeroplanes turned over our own line going east on reconnaissance work. The trenches at Lower Donnet are being deepened throughout improved in view of the number of casualties there. Mairie see. Bm. 29.y."	J.M. Lt. 9.

WAR DIARY / INTELLIGENCE SUMMARY

Army Form C. 2118

Place	Date	Hour	Summary of Events and Information	Remarks and references to Appendices
Trenches S.S. F.1.	18th Jan 1916		In forenoon artillery on both sides was active. The new Tour Aid Post is complete and for some days no air work. One being received. The ax at 131 is being cleaned out to meet as a dressing Post. Is enter to within 150 yards of German sap. From British anxious trench am at 8.30 am. Spring cart Wine S suc. B.29.6"	FRANCE 57 D. S.E. 1/20,000
— do —	19th Jan.		Thiepval was bombarded this afternoon at 11-15 am. One shell burst near Barrow S.C. at noon and nothing heard of R.E. No casualties. Mine Shaft day. Bom. 29.9" facing	
— do —	20th Jan.	at 10.30 am.	6 huns stole from along our wire when by some 200 yards from them when a nice party passed our ready morning. Three of our Aveluy. Heavy one at 8.30 am. Wine Leuilly, about 100yds Gates facing in 132. New rifle-pits are being prepared at Lower Bonnet and Crucifix Corner. Wine Wy S. Jun. Bom. 29.8"	
Bouzincourt	21st Jan.		5th Battn. was relieved today by 11th Border Regt. The relief was complete by 12.15 pm. Three Coys. arrived into billets at Bouzincourt and one Coy. (D) into billets at Aveluy.	
— do —	22nd Jan.		The Battalion rested.	
— do —	23rd.		Divine Service was held at 10.45 am, and then in afternoon Bay. [illegible] have an inter-platoon tug-of-war, recurring was Summer [illegible] in 11 Platoon Keeper Bryan MG. at command (pm 17. Ft.)	

1875 Wt. W593/826 1,000,000 4/15 J.B.C. & A. A.D.S.S./Forms/C.2118.

WAR DIARY or INTELLIGENCE SUMMARY

Army Form C. 2118

Place	Date	Hour	Summary of Events and Information	Remarks and references to Appendices
Bonzincourt	24th Jany		Resting in Bonzincourt. 2 Platoons A Coy. 17" N.F.I.J. sent A Coy 15" N.F.I.J.	
— do —	25th Jany		By 3" Gren. to H.	
— do —	26th Jany		The Divn. Comp. under a month moved to Forceville, 8 miles.	
— do —	27th Jany		Resting and cleaning up. Bombing instruction to selected men. Company instructors and class under orders Lieut. A.G. Lewis slightly wounded by explosion of a detonator.	
Trenches F.L.	28th Jany		J.L. Battalion relieved 11" Border Regiment in F.L. at 2 pm. relief being completed about 3-30 p.m. Enemy fired 35-77mm shells & 14 Minnie Werfers on our line trench 133, damaged parapet returned. Parties home out at night repairing communications. Werfers E, Bay 9, Bm 30."	
— do —	29th Jany		At 1 p.m. enemy shelled new communication trench to 2 turns. At 2.20 p.m. A Battery 161 Bgde. R.F.A. cut wire in front of Drillers — about 150 shells were fired. Parties opened the broken line at night.	
— do —	30th Jany		At 9.20 a.m. enemy working party at broken line was fired on by our guns. All the Companies are engaged repairing temporary trenches. Werfers N.N.E. 35" Bay 9 multi Bm. 30.1" L/C Barnes B.Coy knocked, unwounded. Enemy fired 35"—77mm. Shells and 85 Trench Mortars on our line trenches 131-2,3.	
— do —	31st Jany		At 9.20 to 11 a.m. our guns retaliated at 11 a.m. At 3 p.m. a Somme bombardment started on our right. 18" Divin. shells 60 G.Mm. Henry Seven appear to be mine Werfers E, Bay 9, Bm. 30.2." 17" N.F.I.J. Linking completed in rear by sketcher.	

97th Brigade
32nd Division.

17th BATTALION

HIGHLAND LIGHT INFANTRY

FEBRUARY 1 9 1 6

CONFIDENTIAL.

War Diary
of
17th Bn. A.I.F.

from 1st February, 1916
to 29th February, 1916
(Volume I.)

Army Form C. 2118

WAR DIARY
or
INTELLIGENCE SUMMARY

(Erase heading not required.)

Instructions regarding War Diaries and Intelligence Summaries are contained in F. S. Regs., Part II. and the Staff Manual respectively. Title Pages will be prepared in manuscript.

Place	Date	Hour	Summary of Events and Information	Remarks and references to Appendices

1875 Wt. W 593/826 1,000,000 4/15 J.B.C. & A. A.D.S.S./Forms/C. 2118.

WAR DIARY or INTELLIGENCE SUMMARY

Army Form C. 2118

13

Place	Date	Hour	Summary of Events and Information	Remarks and references to Appendices
Trenches Jelly F.I.	1st Feb		The enemy fired several 5" shells in to our right Coy. Also a new type of trench mortar bomb -3". Our guns fired on a Hun Emplacement at Kimbosyo. 4" Howitzer did little damage and done. One Sub. was killed & two wounded during day. Wenzler 2nd Lieut. Bn. 30.	
	2nd Feb		About 20-77mm shells fell in our front line killing two men, wounding another. On 8" Howitzer fired on above Hun Emplacement placing our shell inside. Hun also active. Damaged enemy line on our left. At night the working parties to cut across the Enemy Wire & some F Sectors guns were silent. The enemy made a 900 yard and the longest communication trench about 350 yards. Of the new front line 700 yards were cut by us and 200 yards by the 18th Division. At 6.15 p.m. a Covering Party, B Coy under Major Jones F, extracts out in front. The wiring party of R.E. with two parties of A Coy "were along with front, left 9-30 P.M with digging party of the 9th Brigade almost back. When work ceased at 3 a.m. the front line was about 6' high & 6' wide commencing bivouacs (2) about 6' deep. There was a gap of 200 yards cut to the enemy between us & the 18th Division. There were 2 killed who were on wiring parties. The night was dry with but a S.E. wind blowing. There were some impressions and by Captain	See Appendix I Map of area showing F.I.

Chippendall, 2nd i/c Field Coy RE

JCC/JM
1/1

Army Form C. 2118

WAR DIARY
or
INTELLIGENCE SUMMARY
(Erase heading not required.)

Instructions regarding War Diaries and Intelligence Summaries are contained in F.S. Regs., Part II. and the Staff Manual respectively. Title Pages will be prepared in manuscript.

Place	Date	Hour	Summary of Events and Information	Remarks and references to Appendices
Trenches F.1.	3 July		In forenoon the enemy gun reported on the new hotel which have been showed quite down by strong parties. During day a enemy gun remained in new hotel masking our view on from trench. At dusk work was resumed as usual & to be stopped at midnight. Weather clear. Any. Bar. 29.5" Freezing.	
do	4 July		At 1 a.m. a salvo of 77mm shells accompanied by Machine Gun fire was directed on new hotel for some 5 minutes. The garrison lying well down weather without casualties. In afternoon our guns fired on Thiepval, Ovillers and La Boisselle sent aim in answer. In two or wounded.	
Avelvy	5 July		The Battalion was relieved in early morning by 11th Border Reg. The relief was complete by 8 a.m. with one man wounded. We were in billets at Avelvy and commenced cleaning kiting. One NCO & 19 men found as first reinforcements.	
do	6 "		The Battalion received clothing by Companies. The village was shelled intermittently from in fire.	
do	7 "			
do	8 "		Very stormy all day alternating between sun & rain in a fierce storm of F.2. At 5:30 the Battalion "stood to". At 6:15 the Coys. advanced out to their respective places in the Bridge Head Defence. Labyrinth, Riseco. 6" was buy were open during the phenomena were Sap Thiepval. No attack developed & at 8:30 the	

1875 Wt. W593/826 1,000,000 4/15 J.B.C. & A. A.D.S.S./Forms/C. 2118.

WAR DIARY or INTELLIGENCE SUMMARY

Army Form C. 2118

15.

Place	Date	Hour	Summary of Events and Information	Remarks and references to Appendices
Avelwy.	9th Feb. (contin.)		Battalion returned to Avelwy, leaving 4 sections in F.2. to reinforce the garrison there morning.	
— do —	10th Feb.		The vicinity was shelled in afternoon. 1 O.R. was wounded.	
Trenches F.1.	11th Feb.		Capt. W.C.O. and 24 men returned from 1st Reinforcement & a further damaged. The Battalion relieved 11th Border Reg. in F.1., relief completed by 12 noon. Lieut. J.B. MacBrayne, R. munro M.O. Ewen Officer wounded slightly on duty. H.E. shell fire around right Coy from Post Donnet in forenoon, no damage done. Annie S.E., morning, Bar. 29.1".	
— do —	12th Feb.		Lower Donnet was shelled by Huniligers in forenoon, no damage done. Our own company in places. The trenches are very wet and our company in places. Westhgasell morning, Bar 29.8"	
— do —	13th Feb.		Owing to wet and enemy shells have been heavier than 77mm. A mine explosion on our right at 12.20 a.m. Dry again.	
— do —	14th Feb.		At 2.15 a.m. a big wet explosion on 4 min running. 2. Again very wet & cloudy, clearing later, Bar 29.6. Enemy artillery active, ranging over whole sector from Crucifix Corner.	
— do —	15th Feb.		Enemy have been very quiet, a relief seems to have taken place. The trenches work has stopped in, but can be very wet & more of the new lines are open shelter during day. 2nd Lieuts J. McArthur, T.C. McCarthur and C. Dobson joined to Battalion on this date.	J.W.H.H.H. 4

1875. Wt. W593/836. 1,000,000 4/15. J.B.C. & A. A.D.S.S./Forms/C. 2118.

WAR DIARY
INTELLIGENCE SUMMARY
(Erase heading not required.)

Army Form C. 2118

16.

Instructions regarding War Diaries and Intelligence Summaries are contained in F.S. Regs., Part II. and the Staff Manual respectively. Title Pages will be prepared in manuscript.

Place	Date	Hour	Summary of Events and Information	Remarks and references to Appendices
Trenches F.I.	16th Feby.		Again very quiet. One gun shelled Thiepval and Authuille between the villages. Enemy retaliated on front line damaging M.E. Esperance wounding 3 men. Very quiet retiring Bar. 29.1"	
Millencourt	17 Feby.		Pumping night relay two kept work in huts below the Chsee. The hut is muddy, but now floored. The try to keep communication to a depth of 2 or 3 feet. The are two kw improved, the communicating trenches widened, deepened in some places duck-walked. The firing trench is fair, stopped, but is not yet any enough. The Battalion was relieved at noon by the 15th Lanc. Fusiliers. The relief was complete at 4 p.m. Other Battalion were being relieved at Millencourt. The 96th Brigade was relieved by 97th Brigade in F Sector. 2nd Lieut J. McCarthy joined the Battalion from Depot Coy. on 24th Jany. Mr. Michaelson to French Mortar Battery. The Battalion marched relieved. The went supply being defined. This was a difficult journey. The weather is very cold, and a biting wind. Rations came. Hypnos brise and fortress below montmarre ne ich acts very kingmann.	
—do—	18th Feby.			
—do—	19 "			
—do—	20 "			
—do—	21 "			
—do—	22nd Feby.		One Coy. A. has gone to Albert for four days to found night working parties and 100 men & two officers of B Coy. have also gone to found a day working party all below F.I. and across the remainder of	J.M.F.L.?

WAR DIARY
INTELLIGENCE SUMMARY

Army Form C. 2118

Instructions regarding War Diaries and Intelligence Summaries are contained in F. S. Regs., Part II. and the Staff Manual respectively. Title Pages will be prepared in manuscript.

Place	Date	Hour	Summary of Events and Information	Remarks and references to Appendices
Millencourt	22nd Feby (contd)		6th Battalion had a route march. The weather is very cold and snow storms prevail.	
— do —	23rd Feby		Battery relieving men concerned. Bombing Machine Gun instruction, route marches & physical exercises. Went over some new improving roads.	
Henencourt	24th Feby		The Battalion moved on foot from Millencourt to Henencourt making improving roads. 2 Pioneer Coys are to be employed in front of latter village. Another Engineer party.	
— do —	25th Feby		Fatigues continued. Men were still very cold. Frost.	
— do —	26th "		Fatigues continued. Frost until 6 inches of snow. A & B Coys on Battalion from Albert.	
— do —	27th Feby		Divisional services that were being arranged. Men still lying rested exercise.	
— do —	28th Feby		Route march. Bombing Machine Gun instruction continued. Weather still very cold. Main transport vehicles comma mostly snow in last three days.	
Dernancourt	29th Feby		The Battalion moved on afternoon, to Dernancourt via Laneville and Ribemont; Buire arriving at 4 pm. We are now 2 miles south of Albert in 18th Division Area. Came attached to 55th Brigade for one day. The billets are good and men comfortable. A heavy bombardment at 6 to 7 pm. Cannot be heard in any town.	

Instructions regarding War Diaries and Intelligence Summaries are contained in F. S. Regs., Part II. and the Staff Manual respectively. Title Pages will be prepared in manuscript.

WAR DIARY
or
INTELLIGENCE SUMMARY
(Erase heading not required.)

Army Form C. 2118

Appendix I

Place	Date	Hour	Summary of Events and Information	Remarks and references to Appendices

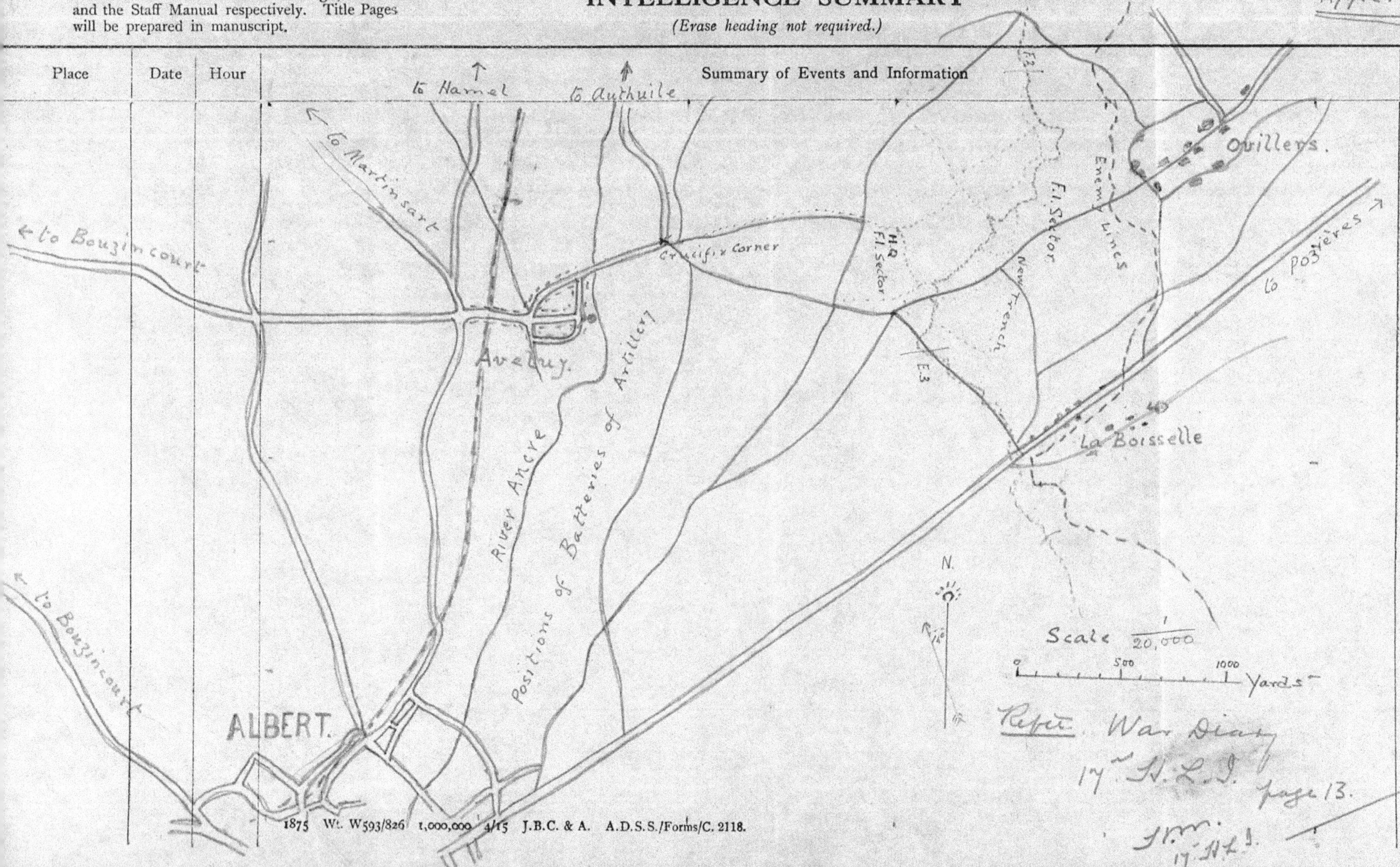

to Hamel
to Authuile
to Martinsart
to Bouzincourt
to Bouzincourt
Crucifix Corner
H.Q F.1. Sector
F.1. Sector
F.2
E.3
New Trench
Enemy Lines
Ovillers.
La Boisselle
to Pozières
Aveluy.
River Ancre
Positions of Batteries of Artillery
ALBERT.
N.
Scale 1/20,000
0
500
1000
Yards

Repeat War Diary 17th H.L.I. page 13.

F.W.M. 17 H.L.I.

1875 Wt. W593/826 1,000,000 4/15 J.B.C. & A. A.D.S.S./Forms/C. 2118.

97th Brigade.

32nd Division.

17th BATTALION

HIGHLAND LIGHT INFANTRY

MARCH 1916

Army Form C. 2118

WAR DIARY
INTELLIGENCE SUMMARY
(Erase heading not required.)

Instructions regarding War Diaries and Intelligence Summaries are contained in F.S. Regs., Part II. and the Staff Manual respectively. Title Pages will be prepared in manuscript.

Place	Date	Hour	Summary of Events and Information	Remarks and references to Appendices
Meynacourt	1st March 1916		The Brigade is still in Divisional Reserve. The 31st Division is taking over from the 18th Division quiet reigns in addition to the F Sector the Sector which lies between the former and Becourt Wood east of Albert. The 14th Brigade are moving out to take over from the 53rd Brigade (18th Division). The other Brigades, 96th are still in the line at F.	
do	2nd Wed		The C.O., Company Commanders & I.O. officers went round the E.1. and sector. A draft of 19 men numerous Divers Others on charge.	
do	3rd		The 97th Brigade relieves the 14th Brigade. The 11th Border Regiment & the 2nd K.O.Y.L.I. take over out sector E.1. and E.2. respectively.	
do	4th		The weather still remains even wit Heavy fires & snow. D Coy are in Reserve at the Becourt Chateau Redoubt, relieving 3rd Coys in E.1. out sector. The Battalions are fairly disposed on arriving at the former, but Games are Played to pass the time.	
do	5th		Divisional services were held for the three Coys.	
do	6th		The weather is much dry & frosty.	
do	7th		C. Coy relieving D Coy in Reserve Coy in Becourt Redoubt.	

J.M. / J.P.J.

Army Form C. 2118

WAR DIARY
INTELLIGENCE SUMMARY
(Erase heading not required.)

Instructions regarding War Diaries and Intelligence Summaries are contained in F.S. Regs., Part II. and the Staff Manual respectively. Title Pages will be prepared in manuscript.

Place	Date	Hour	Summary of Events and Information	Remarks and references to Appendices
Dernancourt	8th Mch.		There is no bathing accommodation in the village. Two boilers have been built up in truck blocks are being made.	
–do–	9."		The work continues any pace.	
Franvillers E.1.	10."		The Battalion relieved with 11th Border Reg. in E.1. at 3 p.m. the relief was complete by 5 p.m. The E sector extends from La Boisselle South to Becourt, roughly – X20 and X26. The 14th Brigade are on our left and the 20th Brigade (7th Division) on our right. The out sector D3 is our right in tier activity by the 2nd Gordons and 2nd Border Reg. The enemy troops is probably there by the 110th Reserve Infantry Regiment & the 28th Reserve Division. (XIV Reserve Corps)	Thob. Ouillers 57 DS E4 10,000
–do–	11."		The front is quiet. The trenches are wet muddy and in several corners of which is active by night. There were several by shrapnel in forenoon. Two Taubes flew over E. Bn 29.1." Patrols were out no unusual one air if men latest events no evidence in X20 d.	
–do–	12."		Our from air exists at X20 d y025, an enemy airient a new type of enemy aeroplane came over lives in forenoon. Army tanks were over at night.	
–do–	13."			
–do–	14."		Our gun out avien at" X26 d 8979. Our –– comm E aberque there was true out of front night. Patrol examined every coon at X20 d 7028. 2nd Lieuts. Drysdale, Alexander von Branton joined.	

1875 Wt. W593/826 1,000,000 4/15 J.B.C. & A. A.D.S.S./Forms/C. 2118.

Army Form C. 2118

WAR DIARY
INTELLIGENCE SUMMARY
(Erase heading not required.)

Instructions regarding War Diaries and Intelligence Summaries are contained in F. S. Regs., Part II. and the Staff Manual respectively. Title Pages will be prepared in manuscript.

Place	Date	Hour	Summary of Events and Information	Remarks and references to Appendices
Trenches E.1.	15th	Md.	Everything quiet on our front. The weather is very bright, warm N.E. 2 winds. Enemy shelled H.Q. at Becourt Chateau & A Coy. Contain one man mortally wounded. More wire just put in front. Some artillery fire on both sides. No damage done to us, but one of the Enemy appears to be knocked out.	
— do —	16th			
Albert	17th		Our guns with heavies fired on Contalmaison. Enemy retaliated on Albert in afternoon wounding two B. our men notably. The 11th Border Reg. relieved the Batt. at 3 p. Shelling was scarce at 5·15 p. The Batt. in reserve trenches at Albert, and one platoon at Tara Redoubt.	
— do —	18th		The town was shelled by 6" shells quite firmly throughout, wounding several civilians and officers. The Batt. is in reserve. Again shelled at 3·15 p.m. and one wounded.	
— do —	19th		— do — two men wounded	
— do —	20th		— do — Our Colonel summoned on tour by officers.	
— do —	21st		Major Paul takes over command of Battalion. Town was shelled at 3·15 p.m. & at 4·15 p.m. Two men wounded.	
— do —	22nd		on Faizgno at La Boisselle	
Trenches E.1.	23rd		at 5 pm. A. Relief started at night to marine army side. The Batt. relieved 11th Border Reg. in E.1. at 3 p.m. Shelling was scarce-	J.M.P.L. 17 J.J.L.

1875 Wt. W593/826 1,000,000 4/15 J.B.C. & A. A.D.S.S./Forms/C. 2118.

WAR DIARY
INTELLIGENCE SUMMARY

Army Form C. 2118

Place	Date	Hour	Summary of Events and Information	Remarks and references to Appendices
Trenches E.1.	24th March		More snow during day. Union N. Bank 29.3". Enemy artillery quieter. Rifle grenades & trench mortars damaged Junior Batt. & many Private Res. Thompson left for Engineers 6.	
—	25"		Telephone Communication. Enemy guns have been more active on our sector than our own. Patrols go out each night and attempt damage the enemy's wire, but have not yet enough to prevent enemy listening.	
—	26"		Our guns cutting gaps in enemy wire at his points. Are just sent new wire on front trench opposite & put on extra support since X.20.1.	
—	27"		Patrol found enemy wire at X20d Y025". Our guns registered on various points. Enemy active at their front trenches in general improving trenches. Are drying out.	
—	28"		A new trench across the enemy re-entrant between X20d and X26 b about 100 yards long was dug during night. The trench 3 ft wide intended to make a cutting-out raid on enemy entrant at X20d Y025	
Dernancourt	29"		went down to Dernancourt to complete their training. The Battalion was relieved by the 11" Border Reg. at 3 pm, & came into billets at Dernancourt, the weather is now much warmer and drying.	

JM
17.3.17

Army Form C. 2118

WAR DIARY
INTELLIGENCE SUMMARY
(Erase heading not required.)

Instructions regarding War Diaries and Intelligence Summaries are contained in F. S. Regs., Part II. and the Staff Manual respectively. Title Pages will be prepared in manuscript.

Place	Date	Hour	Summary of Events and Information	Remarks and references to Appendices
Dernancourt	30 March		Lt. Britton (Cmdr B Coy in place of Lt. Becourt (Colonel) [indecipherable] relieved up. Lewis services to those to be medical were dug into mileage with training get the selects ready, were continued in them. Intake men were to training with 9th raiding party, were guided by Capt. Lewis by special party.	
—	31 March		The special training was continued, observers were kept on look out all day as enemy tried for any new development or regained new lines or enemy trench. The weather is dull & [indecipherable] very overcast.	

Confidential.

War Diary
of
19"(S) B. H.L.I.

Month of March 1916

17/4/1
6. Vol 6
XXXII

WAR DIARY
INTELLIGENCE SUMMARY
(Erase heading not required.)

Army Form C. 2118

Instructions regarding War Diaries and Intelligence Summaries are contained in F.S. Regs., Part II. and the Staff Manual respectively. Title Pages will be prepared in manuscript.

Place	Date	Hour	Summary of Events and Information	Remarks and references to Appendices
Dernancourt	1 April/16		The weather is now very warm & sunny. Observations at the dummy enemy trenches continue. The Battalion are having a good rest.	
" "	2"		A strength of 20 men joined Battalion on 30" March. Two men left for communion. The raid party proceeded to trenches with a view to carrying out the raid ahead with night fairly dark enough. At 11 p.m. a raid of one sergeant & 6 other ranks went over towards the objective X20 c 40 25. At manager crawling with his party took a party of one officer and 3 other ranks went over. About 20 metres tape to indicate route to get in enemy lines. This party were observed when about 20 yards from enemy trench & being fired on were forced to withdraw. Operation were declared off.	
" "	3"		The above party having spent night in Becourt Redoubt left for Dernancourt in afternoon. The trenches having in respect of 2nd night Bombing practice has been carried out east of common water in Becieve.	
Bouzincourt	4"		The Battalion were relieved at 9 p.m. by the 2nd Scottish Rifles, 23rd Brigade, 8th Division. 3rd Corps. The Corps is coming in between the 13th & 10th Corps. Moved in coming in to the march Battalion moved to Bouzincourt Portion into huts vacated by 2nd Inniskillens.	JM.J.Z.9. 17

1875 Wt. W593/826 1,000,000 4/15 J.B.C. & A. A.D.S.S./Forms/C. 2118.

WAR DIARY or INTELLIGENCE SUMMARY

Army Form C. 2118

Place	Date	Hour	Summary of Events and Information	Remarks and references to Appendices
Bouzincourt	5th April 16 to 11th Apl 16		The Battalion worked in trenches, Keeper Trench etc in afternoon. Bombing. Lewis Gun practice, musketry reserve order drill. The weather was very changeable. The men lept ? for Communion on 7th, 9th & 11th.	
Trenches Authuille Subsector	12 Ap.		The Battalion relieved 2nd Manchester Reg. in Authuille Subsector (which was known hence ? (on an inspection as 9.1.) as F2 — 2nd Scottish Rifles, 23rd Brigade, moved up from Becourt. On our left in front of Thiepval is another Battalion of our Brigade 16th H.L.I. The other his Battn on our left — the K.O.Y.L.I, in Authuille and the Border Reg. at Crucifix are in Aveluy. The 96th Brigade is billeted at Contay & the 14th Brigade are at Bouzincourt, Senlis & Warloy. Major J.R. Forsey is in command of Major E. Johnston, 2nd in Command.	
— do —	13 Apl.		The day was quiet on the front. Some lines mortars were sent over by us with every damaging traces of our trains. Aviezig Patrols were sent out at night.	
— do —	14 Apl.		Enemy were more active until 77 mm shells turning Sergt. Robinson and 1 man wounded. 1 man, Lieut. J.S. Pyke-Nott joined Batt. a Lieutenant officer on the — 9 Apr.	

J.M.M.
17.7.17 9.

Army Form C. 2118

WAR DIARY or INTELLIGENCE SUMMARY

(Erase heading not required.)

Place	Date	Hour	Summary of Events and Information	Remarks and references to Appendices
Trenches Authuille Sub-sector	15 Apl. 1916		Arrangements are being made to carry out a raid on enemy trenches until some facility in January or February. The event at R 31 a 4.2 was Lammers fired, observations made on it. Enemy put over some rifle grenades & mortars, we retaliated and 80 rifle grenades Silvers enemy.	
— do —	16"		A quiet day, but one had our men killed at night, D 3 Company in working party.	
Aveluy	17"		The Batt. was relieved in trenches by 2nd Manchesters, 14 Brigade, no 11" Borderers were included in reserve of Messines. The Batt. marched back to Aveluy and dug-outs at Crucifix Corner. L/C Paterson & 3 men left for Commissions. Lieut. P.K.S. Paterson appointed Asst. Adjutant as from 17" March 1916.	
— do —	18"		The Batt. engaged on fatigues, but baths are also available. 16 Eleven transferred from 16" to 17" H.L.I.	
— do —	19" 20"		Enemy were seen digging in Bouzincourt Yard Trenches having gone for the raid on enemy trenches. It is too evident this time to have a Trench artillery bombardment.	J.V.C. 17/3/16

1875 Wt. W593/826 1,000,000 4/15 J.B.C. & A. A.D.S.S./Forms/C. 2118.

Army Form C. 2118

WAR DIARY
or
INTELLIGENCE SUMMARY
(Erase heading not required.)

Instructions regarding War Diaries and Intelligence Summaries are contained in F.S. Regs., Part II. and the Staff Manual respectively. Title Pages will be prepared in manuscript.

Place	Date	Hour	Summary of Events and Information	Remarks and references to Appendices
Trenches Authuille Subsector	21st Apr.		The Batt. relieved 2nd Manchesters in trenches at 8.30 p.m. the relief was complete by 11 P.M.	
— do —	22nd Apr.		Enemy fired over rifle grenades and whizz-bangs in forenoon but no damage done. The raid on the enemy trenches at R31a42 was successfully carried out by Lieuts. Bigg and Campbell & 45 men. Lieut Mackane was in charge of the party with Lying Party. By 9.15 p.m. a white to "tape line" have been laid to 10 yards from enemy wire. Site raiding party have taken up position just outside our wire. At 9.30 to 9.49½ pm, artillery bombard carried out right for ½ minute games down as a barrage. Wire is remaining this movement. Party moved rapidly across, there is remaining the ends and Ammonal torpedo, german was killed. They returned at 10.15 pm. At about this time bombardment on 13 Trenches having resulted bomber came & dug-outs out distroyed a machine Gun. Our loss 11 wounded including 2nd Lt. my own wounded, mostly wounds by enemys barrage on our trenches. The Batt. lost 3 men killed & 11 wounded during enemy retaliation.	1 P.M. 17

WAR DIARY
INTELLIGENCE SUMMARY

Army Form C. 2118

10.

Place	Date	Hour	Summary of Events and Information	Remarks and references to Appendices
Trenches Authuille Sub Sector	23rd Apl.		Lieut. Bigg was found to be severely wounded on No Man's Land. Enemy fired 10.5 c.m. shells along our 2nd line, but our garrison the trenches took over under two hours. We want to be far from best. No deep trenches are rapidly drying out.	
Bouzincourt	24 Apl		Parties were out each night to find ground retaken. They visited our various entries support in No Mans Land by the enemy. Batt. was received by the 2nd Inniskillen Fusiliers 96th Brigade, went into billets in Bouzincourt.	
do	25 Apl		Battalion resting from fatigues.	
do	26 "		do Lewis gun and bombing courses 2nd Lieuts Herron and Henderson former Battere.	
do	27 "		As above. One man wounded slightly on bombing course. The Munster's Instructor being Lieut. C.O., Coy Commanders, 2 Lieutenant officers & 4 N.C.Os. Pur Coy attended a Divisional demonstration near Bazieux.	
do	26 "		Fatigues various. On course, German attacked a Flammenwerfer & others at Senlis & former, various other attempts a German Line in Spring.	17. N. L. D.

1875 Wt. W593/826 1,000,000 4/15 J.B.C. & A. A.D.S.8/Forms/C. 2118.

WAR DIARY
INTELLIGENCE SUMMARY
(Erase heading not required.)

Army Form C. 2118

11.

Place	Date	Hour	Summary of Events and Information	Remarks and references to Appendices
Bouzincourt	29 April 1916	—	The weather is still very fine here must this dried up. Enemy aircraft were so frequent much as never during this Thursday.	
—do—	30	—	A violent thunderstorm over Bouzy river to Thursday which however done damage. Divine service was held in open air at 6 p.m. A few shells fired on outskirts of village in forenoon.	JM. 17/11/16

Confidential.

War Diary
of
17" (S) B. H.L.I.
April 1916.

97th Brigade.

32nd Division.

17th BATTALION

HIGHLAND LIGHT INFANTRY

M A Y 1 9 1 6

Army Form C. 2118

12

WAR DIARY
INTELLIGENCE SUMMARY
(Erase heading not required.)

Instructions regarding War Diaries and Intelligence Summaries are contained in F. S. Regs., Part II. and the Staff Manual respectively. Title Pages will be prepared in manuscript.

Place	Date	Hour	Summary of Events and Information	Remarks and references to Appendices
Bouzincourt	1 May 1916		An aeroplane dropped three bombs on village at 4 a.m. doing no damage. They are free in a fuse. A party of officers, men representing the Battalion attended a Divisional lecture afternoon division to our third on 27" instr.	
	2"		The weather is rather wet, fine. Lewis guns will take out wire barricades.	
	3"		The Ramos retired today. Got our commanding from Major W. J. Paul.	
	4"		A fairly series of operations at Bazieux to be today free in morning no names stated. Some of the missing party went to Martinsart & was about our the guns general tune of D Battery 168 Brigade R.F.A. They were also about as 4.5" and 8" Grenages.	
Rubempré	5"		The Brigade marched back today being relieved by the XIV" Brigade. The 19" Lancashire Fusiliers with our fires on at Bouzincourt at 3.30p attempted the Battalion marched 11 miles to billets in Rubempré 9 miles N. of E. of Amiens arriving about 9 p.m. Major Brown, Ryecroft, Lieut. the march from with Battalion marching through Senlis.	
	6"		The Battalion rested. A draft of 30 men arrived on 6" inst.	
	7"		Divine service was held at 10.30 a.m. Bombing Course civilized unwise various and brass inspection. Their were now of for Commander on 2 was of.	
	8"		Bombing musketry occur and drill in Forenoon.	Nos. 17/M.F.S.

Army Form C. 2118

/3

WAR DIARY
INTELLIGENCE SUMMARY
(Erase heading not required.)

Instructions regarding War Diaries and Intelligence Summaries are contained in F. S. Regs., Part II. and the Staff Manual respectively. Title Pages will be prepared in manuscript.

Place	Date	Hour	Summary of Events and Information	Remarks and references to Appendices
Rubempré	9th May 1916		The Battalion marched 6 miles to Dernancourt having gone west of Bazieux, present through small openings as previously. Limbs hands were in as cave the ammo.	
"do"	10th May		Bowling, working, marching, machine gun course in forenoon. Capt Gardner talks to Machine Gun Corps. Breakfasts as from 28th April.	
"do"	11th "		The Battalion took part in the Brigade Divisional Field exercises near Baizieux.	
"do"	12th "			
"do"	13th "		The following decorations have been awarded the Battalion:– Military Cross – Lieuts. Begg and Carpenter. D.C.M. – Sergt. Major Reith, B.Coy. Military Medal – Sergt. Taylor, Private Leiper and Macintosh. The Battalion Sports were commenced in afternoon but postponed on account of rain. Limber officers attended a Divine Service and Dernancourt night marching concerned on account of long rain. Sports here in late afternoon.	
"do"	14th "			
"do"	15th "		marches, Machine Gun, Bowling re-commenced	

JMcM.
17.N.2.9.

WAR DIARY
INTELLIGENCE SUMMARY

Army Form C. 2118

14.

Place	Date	Hour	Summary of Events and Information	Remarks and references to Appendices
Rubempré	16th May	—	Bn. moved into new Divisional Area. Nothing unusual.	
Warloy	17"	—	At 2 p.m. the Battalion left for Warloy en route for front area. Ground was difficult then for our night.	
Aveluy	18"	—	At 7 p.m. the Battalion left for Aveluy marching by Platoons. Enemy was fairly quiet. Three Coys. are dug in at Crucifix Corner, one Coy. the Battalion is in Brigade reserve.	
— do —	19"	—	The whole Battalion is engaged on the Working Parties in front area. A draft of 13 men arrived.	
— do —	20"	—	Two men wounded near Authuille.	
— do —	21st	—	One man wounded.	
Trenches Authuille Sub sec 47	22nd	—	In evening relieved 11th Border Regt. in front line. The relief was quiet. Relief was complete at 11 p.m.	
— do —	23rd	—	Enemy were active on our right during our heads mortars of all kinds — whizzbangs & minenwerfer — gassing limbers considerably. Shells are being cut in Communication Trenches to provide shelter in bombardment. New trenches are being dug behind fire trench as these in existence are unknown.	One J.P.M. 14/ 14"/14/J

WAR DIARY / INTELLIGENCE SUMMARY

Army Form C. 2118

15.

Place	Date	Hour	Summary of Events and Information	Remarks and references to Appendices
Trenches Authuille Sub-sector	24th May 1916		In forenoon 77mm shells burst all over trenches, our guns retaliated. One man wounded.	
— do —	25th May		Enemy trench mortars very active on our right in early morning following up by any artillery fire on trenches was continuing. Heavy guns were in action also our Stokes Guns. The trenches are in a bad state. Plowed in many parts. Sky are again enjoying it. One man wounded & 3 shellshock. Heavy shells fire throughout day namely 13.N.Q from Authuille, mostly 15 cm. and 10.2 cm. Very little damage done. In afternoon our right even heavily shelled, hour mortars retaliated. Part of Trench have been in, or occupant 6 men shell shock. The back were relieved in the evening by 11th Bombay Reg. relief was complete by 11 pm. Three Coys. N.Q. moved to dug-outs at Crucifix Corner. & one Coy to billets in Aveluy. During this time there with the enemy there one must more than usual more than usual in some trenches opposite our lines for our casualties were very slight.	
Crucifix Corner	26th			17.J.H.Q.

Army Form C. 2118

16.

WAR DIARY
INTELLIGENCE SUMMARY
(Erase heading not required.)

Place	Date	Hour	Summary of Events and Information	Remarks and references to Appendices
Crucifix Corner	27th May 1916		The enemy sunk ten or eleven trench mortar shells in his lines along the Aveluy-Authuille Road. He also Trench M. is engaged on working parties in the trenches opposite at Aveluy. He shows increased activity generally on the river Ancre.	
— do —	28th		The Battalion is engaged on working parties. Three men were wounded in these trenches. The Revd. Chaplain Capt. A.N. Bay has been posted to 17th H.L.I. from 16th H.L.I. and R.C. Chaplain, Capt. R. de Martin, has been posted to 16th H.L.I. from 17th H.L.I.	
	29th			
	30th			
Warloy	31st May		The Battalion were relieved about midnight 30/31st May by Br. 16th Lancashire Fusiliers & marched to billets in Warloy arriving about 3 a.m. The Brigade is in Divisional Reserve. The Battalion has been posted as "available" from 29th May.	17th H.L.I.

97th Brigade.
32nd Division.

1/17th BATTALION

HIGHLAND LIGHT INFANTRY

JUNE 1916

WAR DIARY or INTELLIGENCE SUMMARY

Army Form C. 2118
32/
17.4
17 HLI
Vol 8

Place	Date	Hour	Summary of Events and Information	Remarks and references to Appendices
WARLOY	1st June		The Battalion took part in Divisional Tactical Exercise on BAIZIEUX Training Ground. Hostile Tank experiment at SENLIS.	
	2nd June		Company training – Bombing, musketry, physical training Lewis and S.A.A. Gun's carried. The Battalion has been mentioned in General Sir Douglas Haig's dispatch.	
	3rd June		Company training – do – do – do – do	
	4th June		At Church Parade – Major General W.H. Rycroft presented Ribbons to Lieutenant R.J. Begg, 2nd Lieutenant J.H. Carpenter. No.15507 C.S.M. S.A. Reith, 15458 Sergt. A.J. Taylor, 13720 Private D. McIntosh. The G.O.C. announced that temporary Lieutenant Colonel A.S. Morton V.D. had been awarded the Companionship of the Order of St. Michael and St George.	
	5th June		Company training continued.	
	6th June		Divisional Area Hors at the Battalion's Disposal but no Sports to interest exercise.	
	7th June		Company training Continued. 2300 Private H.R. Vint "B" Company returned to England for a Commission. 2nd Lieutenant A. Macleod has left for Instruction prior to a Staff appointment.	
	8th June		The Battalion took part in Divisional Tactical Exercise at BAIZIEUX. 2nd Lieut. D.G. Morgan joins the Battalion today and now posts to "A" Company. 2nd Lieut. J.M. McArthur, di. transferred from "A" to "D" Company.	

WAR DIARY or INTELLIGENCE SUMMARY

Army Form C. 2118

Place	Date	Hour	Summary of Events and Information	Remarks and references to Appendices
WARLOY.	9th June		Company training – continued.	
	10th June		Owing to bad weather Church Parade was cancelled. Lieut-Colonel O.J. Morton L.Mcl. L.B. left for course of instruction at the 4th Army School FLIXECOURT. Major W.J. Paul proceeded to leave and Major J.R. Young resumed command of the Battalion.	
	11th June			
CONTAY.	12th June		The 32nd & 5th Divisions had a combined field day at BAIZIEUX. The 14th Brigade supported the 96th Brigade in Divisional Reserve. The Battalion went into Camp in CONTAY WOOD, the 16th H.L.I. and 2nd K.O.Y.L.I. are also in the wood. The 11th Borders are billeted in CONTAY. The weather is very hot and the Camp in a very bad state. This was the earliest move to have had so far.	
	13th June		Captain H.H. Morton took over command of Brigade Musketry and Bombing School in CONTAY. Lieutenants A.J.S. Brevret and O.P. Symington and four N.C.Os attending for instruction. The Companies have commenced special training of Bombers – Throwers – Messengers – Snipers etc. Two 150 men for fatigue daily.	

WAR DIARY or INTELLIGENCE SUMMARY

Army Form C. 2118

Place	Date	Hour	Summary of Events and Information	Remarks and references to Appendices
CONTAY.	14th June		Company training continued.	
	15th June		The 32nd & 38th Divisions had combined exercise at BAIZIEUX.	
	16th June		Company training continued.	
	19th June		Lieut Col. O.C. Morton. C.M.G. V.D. returned from FLIXECOURT. 2nd Lieut. A.G. Marshall joined the Battalion and was posted to C Company.	
	18th June		Company training continued. Church Parade was held in the wood at 6.30pm.	
	19th June		Company parade.	
	20th June		Company training continued. A Brigade Concert was held in the wood.	
	21st June		The Battalion took part in Divisional Tactical Exercises on the Belincourt - Baizieux area. In the evening the Raiders held their dinner at the Hotel Moderne - Contay.	
	22nd June		Company training continued. A reinforcement of 1 officer 8 other ranks were posted to the Battalion on the 20th inst. 2nd Lieut. Blake and Jones to A Coy. 2nd Lieut. Kirk and King to B. Coy. 2nd Lieut. Brown and McLeod to C Coy. 2nd Lieut. McConnell & Laurie to D Coy. The Battn. moved from Contay Wood to Warloy at 10pm.	

WAR DIARY or INTELLIGENCE SUMMARY

Army Form C. 2118

Place	Date	Hour	Summary of Events and Information	Remarks and references to Appendices
Warloy	23rd June		The Battalion moved to Senlis after church – the route taken was a very circuitous one. Stables were transferred from G.C. at Senlis. New Company arrangements made under Company arrangements.	
Senlis	24th		Church Parade was held in the open at 10 a.m. – Cpl. Chapman was promoted to a Commission and posted to the Batt. as Intelligence Officer from the 28th inst.	
	25th		Companies went out route marching.	
	26th			
Bouzincourt	27th		The Battalion moved to Bouzincourt by night. The Companies to billets – the transport to lines S. of the Albert-Rens road. Being the very hot weather the Batt. did not move into its new alignment as originally was intended. The relief was to be made 48 hours later. Bouzincourt was shelled at 2 A.M. Killing one tramping one of our rations cart horses. The Coys did physical training and bayonet fighting practice.	
	28th			
	29th			
	30th		Bouzincourt was shelled during the day we had 2 men wounded. The Battalion moved into the line and took up the Battle positions. We had no casualties when moving up.	

[signed] Capt.

July Vol 9

Confidential

War Diary

of 17th (S) Battn H.L.I

From 1st July 1916 to 31st July 1916.

J.A. Halliday, Captain,
Adjutant, 17th (S) Bn H.L.I.

WAR DIARY or INTELLIGENCE SUMMARY

(Erase heading not required.)

Army Form C. 2118

Instructions regarding War Diaries and Intelligence Summaries are contained in F.S. Regs., Part II. and the Staff Manual respectively. Title Pages will be prepared in manuscript.

Place	Date	Hour	Summary of Events and Information	Remarks and references to Appendices
Trenches British and German	July 1	12.30 A.M.	A Coy report explosion of Mortars Bomb Store which caused 13 casualties - including C.S.M. Roth - all wounds. In addition B Coy had 6 men wounded thro' shell fire about this time. Zero time was fixed for 7.30 A.M. This time communicated to Coy Commanders but the men were not told until after daylight.	
		7.23 A.M.	A & B Coy starts crawling across "No mans Land". D & C Coy waits till 16th H.L.I. and A Coy 16th H.L.I. advance of our B Coy. This Coy of 16th then only two yards out got severely dealt with by enemy machine guns, tho' two platoons got up to the wire then found the latter very strong wire. Lieut. McLaren and a few men joined our B Coy and eventually proved to be the only men of 16th H.L.I. to penetrate the enemy line.	
		7.30 A.M.	18 pounders Barrage lifted and our men entered the enemy front line. The entry lines proved on which the magsons proceeded to clear to dugouts. A number of prisoners were taken. The advance across the open was splendidly carried out all ranks behaved magnificently - to assist us the Casl throughout the entire action. Captain Mitchell and 2nd Lieutenant Beckett were both wounded before reaching the enemy front trenches	

WAR DIARY or INTELLIGENCE SUMMARY

Army Form C. 2118

Place	Date	Hour	Summary of Events and Information	Remarks and references to Appendices
	1/7/16	8 A.M.	was Lieut. Miller on the right of C Company. Leipzig Trench was taken and the enemy line advanced against Hindenburg Trench. These trenches were mown down and by 8.15 A.M. every Company Officer was a casualty. The 2nd K.O.Y.L.I. came up but did not go beyond Leipzig Trench. It now became obvious to Col. Martin that Leipzig Trench must be held to without reinforcement no further advance could be made but flanks being exposed as the 8th Division on our right had been driven back. The left was particularly exposed and parties under Sergt. Macgregor and Sergt. Pratt were organised and sent to every Pow. to left as left centre respectively. When B & D Coys. had been almost annihilated. Our casualties now amount to 22 Officers and 500 other ranks.	
		9.30 A.M.	The 11th & 12th Border Regt. debouched from Authuille Wood and were absolutely wiped out by enemy machine gun fire from the valley E. of the wood very heavily.	

WAR DIARY or INTELLIGENCE SUMMARY

Army Form C. 2118

(Erase heading not required.)

Instructions regarding War Diaries and Intelligence Summaries are contained in F. S. Regs., Part II. and the Staff Manual respectively. Title Pages will be prepared in manuscript.

Place	Date	Hour	Summary of Events and Information	Remarks and references to Appendices
	1/7/16	9-40 A.M.	Our bombers were holding the flanks successfully, the bomb supply was excellent. The bombers under 2nd Lieut. Morrison being extremely responsible for this.	
		10-10 A.M.	The Brigade were not to push on when the guns lifted off Trönesburg Trench, but the scramble on our left made this movement impossible unless it was in Trönesburg Trench and in spite of persistent bombing we were unable to take it.	
		11-15 A.M.	The flanks still held but the Entire line very weak.	
		12 noon	The Worcesters came up on our right flank and relieved the tension there. A forward movement was attempted by them, but was delayed by no not- the trench we unable to make any progress.	
		12-38 P.M.	2nd Manchester Regt. got orders to attack Trönesburg Trench.	
		2-11 P.M.	Situation was still unchanged, bombing parties works had 2nd Lieut Morrison and Moss worked throughout all the ordeal with untiring courage and without the least regard of personal safety and to them is due the little organisation	

1875 Wt. W593/826 1,000,000 4/15 J.B.C. & A. A.D.S.S./Forms/C. 2118.

Army Form C. 2118

WAR DIARY
or
INTELLIGENCE SUMMARY

(Erase heading not required.)

Instructions regarding War Diaries and Intelligence Summaries are contained in F.S. Regs., Part II. and the Staff Manual respectively. Title Pages will be prepared in manuscript.

Place	Date	Hour	Summary of Events and Information	Remarks and references to Appendices
	10/9/16	3.45 P.M.	of the position which kept our line against enemy launching counter attacks.	
			The 8th asks no far information of 16th Hy. Bde location.	
		4-7 P.M.	The 2nd Manchesters reinforced our flanks with one Company on each. This greatly relieved our left which had been badly threatened. Just at this time our line moved a little to the centre but control was momentarily lost. The large number of men of other units without officers & NCOs made control very difficult.	
		4-15 P.M.	Situation critical.	
		4-20 P.M.	8th who appreciating our desperate position but urge no return to the Manchester Trench assistance in reformed movement.	
		4-47 P.M.	Manchesters in position on our flanks but all idea of forward movement given up.	
		4-55 P.M.	Ordered to consolidate ground taken.	

WAR DIARY or INTELLIGENCE SUMMARY

Army Form C. 2118.

Place	Date	Hour	Summary of Events and Information	Remarks and references to Appendices
	July 1/16		In the evening the enemy again delivered two strong counter-attacks, which were, however, easily repulsed by our men. At 9.30 we began to be relieved by two companies of the Lancashires, but the relief was not wholly carried out until near midnight. In addition to the Lancashires, a hundred men from the K.O.Y.L.I.s were sent as reinforcements. The majority of our battalion were relieved by 11.30 pm, but several hunting parties belonging to the 17th were made to be relieved till well on toward mid day of the following day. The 17th fell back on Lanspau Post, and took their in that sub-sector. ⟨sgd⟩	
Reserve Trenches	July 2/16		Most of our men spent the night in Kintyre Trench, and Blackett St. In the morning a roll-call was taken, and inquiries made about the missing. Carrying parties were required to take water to our advanced posts. We sustained a few casualties in our trenches through shell-fire. In the evening the Battalion was relieved and returned to the cuirs at Ouderdom.	

WAR DIARY or INTELLIGENCE SUMMARY

Army Form C. 2118

Place	Date	Hour	Summary of Events and Information	Remarks and references to Appendices
Crucifix Corner	July 3.16		Battalion resting for day at Crucifix Corner. Suffered S.A.A and grenades returned to Stores at Crucifix Corner. Major Paul rejoins Battn. after temporary indisposition. Information being collected about casualties. Killed in action on 1.7.16:- Major Mitchison, Capts. Boyd & Steele, Lieuts. MacBrayne, Symington, Maxwell, Gillie, 2nd Lieuts. Laird, Alexander, Younge, Carpenter, Bruston. The Wounded Officers include Major Long, Capts. Mitchell & Russell, Lieuts. Begg, Miller, 2nd Lieuts. Beckett, McLaurie, McArthur, Elwood, Chapman. Temporary Commands:- Capt. Ingram to D.Coy (2.7.16); 2nd Lieut. Harrison to A.Coy (2.7.16); 2nd Lieut. Harris to B.Coy (2.7.16); In evening of this date the Battn. moves back to Contay Wood.	
Contay Contay	July 4.16 July 5.16		Contay Wood: Battalion parades for rolls-calls. Total Casualties- 447 (other Ranks), Officers 22. Contay Wood: Examination of kits of deceased & wounded men; personal effects collected for sending from Battalion have bath at Contay.	

Place	Date	Hour	Summary of Events and Information	Remarks and references to Appendices
Contay	July 1.17		Contay Wood: Company training. Received following message from the King to Sir D. Haig:- "Please convey to the Army under your command my sincere congratulations on the results achieved in the recent fighting. I am proud of my troops. No one could have fought more bravely. (sgd.) George R.)	
Contay	July 7.17		Contay Wood: Company training. In the evening the Bn. paraded to Senlis when they drew grenades & iron rations.	
Senlis	July 8.17		Senlis: We are under orders to go into the trenches tonight. In the afternoon the Bn. paraded for the last time under Colonel Heaton, who is about to return from active service in the field. The Colonel addressed the men, congratulating them in warm fitting terms for their devotion while under his command and wishing them well in the vicissitudes of the future. Major Paul on behalf of the Battalion, extended their fund respect to officers, non-commissioned officers & men in having the guidance & leadership of Colonel Heaton, who has raised the Battalion to such a high stage of proficiency. We wish the	

WAR DIARY
or
INTELLIGENCE SUMMARY

(Erase heading not required.)

Army Form C. 2118

Place	Date	Hour	Summary of Events and Information	Remarks and references to Appendices
British Trenches			Colonel a well wounded sent out and all happiness. Major Paul takes on the command of the Battalion.	
"	July 9.16		In the evening we move into the trenches - Hqrs at Quarry Post - in support to 7th K.O.Y.L.I.	
"	July 10.16		The Trenches; In reserve at Quarry Post.	
"	July 11.16		The Trenches; The Battn relieve the 2nd Border Reg. at Consohn St. Telegram J. cange's chothan are received from the G.O.C. X Corps. thro' O.C. 32nd Division. New trench is commenced between Stanley St. and Rivington St. N19076 L.I. employing 2 officers & 120 men. Regimental orders deprecate at Quarry Post.	
"	July 12.16		The Trenches. Digging new trench.	
"	July 13.16		The Trenches. A bombing party of about 100 men was asked for, to attack the German trenches + trench Harrow + Kirk. left our trenches after dusk taking the rd. leading toward dragoon + Kents Harrow + Kirk. left our trenches after dusk taking the rd. leading toward the Inniskilling trenches. The party, under Captain H. Innes Kelling, Inniskilling Fusiliers at 11.45 pm in conjunction with the Inniskillings they	

WAR DIARY or INTELLIGENCE SUMMARY

Army Form C. 2118

Place	Date	Hour	Summary of Events and Information	Remarks and references to Appendices
Bulah Trenches.	July 3./16 (Ctd)		Opened bombing attack on the Germans on their left, drove them out of their trenches. Unfortunately Captain Simpson was mortally wounded at the outset, and 2nd Lieuts Nevin & Kirk were rendered "hors de combat". A party of Engineers accompanied our men for the purpose of constructing barriers in the captured trench. Before dawn the enemy counter-attacked and retook the trenches. Our casualties amounted to about 50% of the whole party. They were relieved at 6 a.m. Total Casualties up to date :- Killed 85 O.R., Missing 98 O.R., Wounded 308 O.R. Shellshock 14 O.R. Died of Wounds 14 O.R.	
"	July 4./16.		The trenches; Burying parties clear the dead from the trenches in our sub-sector.	
"	July 5./16.		Battalion is relieved by 4th Gloucesters at 1 a.m. and proceed to huts in Bouzincourt. Casualties to date :- Killed 90, Missing 85, Wounded 323. Total 498 O.R. Strength of Battn. = 466 O.R.	

Army Form C. 2118.

WAR DIARY
or
INTELLIGENCE SUMMARY

(Erase heading not required.)

Instructions regarding War Diaries and Intelligence Summaries are contained in F. S. Regs., Part II. and the Staff Manual respectively. Title Pages will be prepared in manuscript.

Place	Date	Hour	Summary of Events and Information	Remarks and references to Appendices
Ancre.	July 16/7/16.		Brigade under orders to move to Amplier. Battalion parade at 2.30 & proceed via Acheux. Beauvincourt Leaton. Halt for tea outside Beauvincourt. Whole brigade in huts at Amplier. Weather conditions are bad: poured in rain fall all night; many of the huts are flooded out.	
Lus St Leger	July 18/7/16.		Brigade move into area about Lus St Leger. Bath parade in afternoon to be addressed by Gen Rycroft, who congratulates the Brigade on their work in the trenches. Thereafter we leave for Lus St Leger, via Halley Luckerne, where we had for tea. Reach Lus about 8 pm. Find comfortable billets.	
"	July 19/7/16.		Lus St Leger: Rest for day here.	
Tornas.	July 19/7/16.		Battn leaves for Tornas via Beauincourt, Elue, Henin, Thoavel. Weather is good, roads dry. Packs are carried; no transport being available.	

Army Form C. 2118.

WAR DIARY
or
INTELLIGENCE SUMMARY
(Erase heading not required.)

Instructions regarding War Diaries and Intelligence Summaries are contained in F. S. Regs., Part II. and the Staff Manual respectively. Title Pages will be prepared in manuscript.

Place	Date	Hour	Summary of Events and Information	Remarks and references to Appendices
Jangry	July 20/7/16		Under order to move to Jangry. Battalion proceeds by Ostreville, Boyas, and Nœuxnoom, arriving in time for dinner. Good billets and found. Lieut Bigg & 2nd Lieut Buckett have succumbed to their wounds.	
Allonagne	July 21/7/16		Moving again. Jangry to Allonagne, via Auchel and Rozynghem. Weather still good. Battalion comfortably billetted by 2 p.m. Kiss addr-aktions join us in evening :- 2nd Lieuts Nielson, Hackett, Barclay, Mabeli. 2nd Lieuts McGlashan, Mason, Breslin, Brown, Duncan - to Z Coy.	
"	July 22/7/16		Allonagne : 99th Brigade in billets here. Inspection of Companies.	
"	July 23/7/16		Allonagne : Church Parade at 10·30. Arrival of four more subalterns :- 2nd Lieuts Duncommi, Dewar, Paterson, Wollen. Messrs Duncommi Paterson to Y Coy. Messrs Dewar & Wollen to Z Coy.	

WAR DIARY
or
INTELLIGENCE SUMMARY

(Erase heading not required.)

Army Form C. 2118.

Place	Date	Hour	Summary of Events and Information	Remarks and references to Appendices
Allouagne	July 24.16		Allouagne: Company training in morning. Brigade bombing courses in Trigonometry.	
Allouagne	July 25.16		Battalion has baths. Companies parade for Coy training at 9.30 a.m. Brigade bombing school continues. Two orders parade for motorisation riding under Transport Officer. A Routine Order is issued published in regarding the illegal defacing by soldiers of government Property.	
Allouagne – Bethune	July 26.16		Brigade moves to Bethune. Battalion leaves Allouagne at 10. a.m. and proceed via Pont de Rivellon and Chaques. Battalion bathing party under her Doran leaves at 7 a.m. Battn arrives at Bethune about 1 p.m., and along with the 76th H.L.I. are quartered in the "Orphelinat", Rue des ____	
Bethune	July 27.16		Company training continues during forenoon. Men had swimming-baths. Issue of new clothes to a large number of the Battalion.	

2449 Wt. W14957/M90 750,000 1/16 J.B.C. & A. Forms/C.2118/12.

WAR DIARY or INTELLIGENCE SUMMARY

Army Form C. 2118.

Place	Date	Hour	Summary of Events and Information	Remarks and references to Appendices
Bethune	July 28/16		14th & 197th Brigades were inspected by General Munro, Commanding 1st Army, at J.6 a.7.? near Labussière. Battalion left Bethune about 1 pm, in full marching order with helmets, reaching parade ground about 2.15 pm. Inspection took place at 3 pm. First line transport attached. The day was very warm.	
"	July 29/16		Company training and bathing. Courses opened in bombing, Lewis Gun, Anti-Gas, Bombs dropped in town by enemy aeroplanes.	
"	July 30/16		Church Parade at 9 am. Communion was also held. Pte Broadhurst 1 Wood J.C. Coy. proceed to England - these are shaini lite. 8 letters to a common war Infection by Commanding Officer of Battalion at 12 noon.	
"	July 31/16		Battalion paraded for route march to Annequin at 5.30 am. W15423 Pte D.A.Rogers. C Coy. proceeded to Brown and other hostas (30.7.16 - 6.8.16) & No 2870 Pte John D Coy to course in Cookery @ 2 am Javed. Courses continue here on Signalling, Lewis Gun, Bombing, Anti-Gas, musketry. Company training. Subalterns parade under R.S.M. and Adjutant.	

2449 Wt. W14957/M90 750,000 1/16 J.B.C. & A. Forms/C.2118/12.

Confidential
War Diary
of 17th. B. H.L.I.
from 1st July 1916. to 31st July 1916

(Sgd) C. McCallum.

Vol 10

Confidential

War Diary

of

17th (S) Bn. Highland Light Infantry.

from 1st August. 1916   to 31st Aug. 1916

G. K. S. Netherton
Captain & Adjutant

Volume 1

WAR DIARY
or
INTELLIGENCE SUMMARY
(Erase heading not required.)

Army Form C. 2118.

Instructions regarding War Diaries and Intelligence Summaries are contained in F. S. Regs., Part II and the Staff Manual respectively. Title Pages will be prepared in manuscript.

Place	Date	Hour	Summary of Events and Information	Remarks and references to Appendices
BETHUNE.	Aug 1.16		Company Training: Bombing, physical training, bayonet fighting, etc.	
"	Aug 2.16		Battalion parade at 5.30 a.m. for route march to FOUQUEREUIL, returning at 7.30 a.m. Forenoon given over to baths in BETHUNE.	
"	Aug 3.16		Sub Battalion parade with crooks etc. in morning and proceed to the rifle range near LABEUVRIÈRE (D.23.B.5.3). Good practice put in at the range, firing from trenches, and under "flat gun" conditions. Company Officers visit the trenches at Cambrin right sub-sector preparatory to taking over. Capt. Evans R.A.M.C. goes on sick leave on release by Lieut. Biddle R.A.M.C.	
	Aug 4.16		Early morning route march BETHUNE – VERQUIN – BETHUNE. Forenoon: Coy. training: Baths: instruction in battle order.	
	Aug 5.16		Battalion leaves BETHUNE at 10.30 a.m., proceeding to CAMBRIN right sub-sector, which we take over from the Northampton. Battalion Hqrs are situated at RAILWAY KEEP, later one from one Coy of 1st Sherwoods (Notts and Derbys). 16th 14 L.I. are on our left.	

2449 Wt. W14957/M90 750,000 1/16 J.B.C. & A. Forms/C.2118/12.

Army Form C. 2118.

WAR DIARY
or
INTELLIGENCE SUMMARY
(Erase heading not required.)

Instructions regarding War Diaries and Intelligence Summaries are contained in F. S. Regs., Part II. and the Staff Manual respectively. Title Pages will be prepared in manuscript.

Place	Date	Hour	Summary of Events and Information	Remarks and references to Appendices
TRENCHES (Canbrin st. Sub. Sector).	Aug 6.16		Heavy T.M. Bombardment from the enemy in the early evening. Our losses are two killed and eleven wounded — including Mr. Henderson who was mortally wounded during the performance of his duties as M.G. Officer. MKelly	
	Aug 7.16		T.M.s and rifle grenades again do much damage to our front line and saps, particularly in vicinity of mine-shafts. We have two men wounded and three buried (missing). During the night their bodies are recovered. MKelly	
	Aug 8.16		Very quiet day; we have no casualties. MKelly	
	Aug 9.16		During the day we have the misfortune of losing two men who are done to death in our trenches by a stray party of the enemy who take advantage of the long grass to crawl our unobserved. Our T.M.s and Stokes guns open violent bombardment on the enemy lines. Wiring is done at Railway Kep by Italian garrisoning. MKelly Draught of 200 Highland Cycle Brigade arrive to join us	

2449 Wt. W4957/M90. 750,000 1/16 J.B.C. & A. Forms/C.2118/12.

WAR DIARY
INTELLIGENCE SUMMARY
(Erase heading not required.)

Army Form C. 2118.

Place	Date	Hour	Summary of Events and Information	Remarks and references to Appendices
TRENCHES. (Cambrin ad sec)	Aug 10.16.		Battalion is relieved during the afternoon by 11th Bord. Regiment, and withdrawn to ANNEQUIN. One officer and thirty men are left to garrison Railway Keep. The draught are awaiting our return at Annequin and are drawn up on parade to meet Major Paul.	
ANNEQUIN.	Aug 11.16.		Baths for the Battn. Garrison provided for CARTERS KEEP and CHURCH WEST KEEP. Party of 16 draught furnish fatigue for the trenches. New Clothes are issued	
"	Aug 12.16.		Parade under Company arrangements. Promotion made: Issue of an P.H.G. helmet to every man. Lieut. T. Adj. Patron becomes Capt. and Adj. will effect from 2nd July 16. Major Paul becomes Lieut. Colonel will effect from 30th July 16. 2nd Lieut. Huson Shaw assumes rank of Capt.	

WAR DIARY
or
INTELLIGENCE SUMMARY

(Erase heading not required.)

Army Form C. 2118.

Instructions regarding War Diaries and Intelligence Summaries are contained in F.S. Regs., Part II. and the Staff Manual respectively. Title Pages will be prepared in manuscript.

Place	Date	Hour	Summary of Events and Information	Remarks and references to Appendices
ANNEQUIN	Aug 13.16		Coy training; bombing etc. [signed]	
"	Aug 14.16		Trenches; late news from Border Regiment again in CAMBRIN right sub-sector. Relief carried out quietly at 2 p.m. In the evening our trenches were badly damaged and our safe blown in, causing four deaths, one wounded, and fourteen wounded. [signed]	
TRENCHES	Aug 15.16		The day is quiet. At 3 p.m. our T.M. and Stokes guns opened rapid bombardment, which lasted for ten minutes. Our trench mortars useful no. Garrison of Borders at no. N4 90 at Red Kite, went in front of the Keep during the night. Riflemen Campbell, from 10th H.L.I., joins the battalion. [signed]	
"	Aug 16.16		Arty and trenches are clearer and days quiet. [signed]	
"	Aug 17.16		At 11.45 - 11.55 our TMs and SKs guns open again after rapid bombardment. No enemy retaliation made. We are relieved at 2 p.m. by 11th Borders and withdraw to Nullagh Lines - Headquarters [signed]	

Army Form C. 2118.

WAR DIARY
or
INTELLIGENCE SUMMARY
(Erase heading not required.)

Instructions regarding War Diaries and Intelligence Summaries are contained in F.S. Regs., Part II. and the Staff Manual respectively. Title Pages will be prepared in manuscript.

Place	Date	Hour	Summary of Events and Information	Remarks and references to Appendices
	Aug 17th (Cntd).		are at Mazum Rouge. Reorganise into four distinct Companies.	
TRENCHES.	Aug 18.16.		We are Battn in Support. Disposn as follows: B Coy in Old Boot Trench, A.C.D Coys in Village trins Hope at Mazum Rouge. (Winchester)	
"	Aug 19.16.		Bn in support: all quiet.	
"	Aug 20.16.		In outpost: quiet day. Sent working parties to front line.	
"	Aug 21.16.		Battn to relieved. We are relieved by 2nd R. Innis. Bns., and withdraw to billets in Beuvry.	
BEUVRY.	Aug 22.16.		Baths. Course in Lewis Guns, dc started. Progress	
"	Aug 23.16.		Battn. has orders to proceed to MAZINGARBE, in aren I. Nelmets lecture. Colonel Paul and Coy Officers visited the trenches at Hulluch Centre Section.	
MAZINGARBE	Aug 24.16.		Battn. takes over trenches from 1st Munster Fusiliers (48th Bde. 16th Division) in	

WAR DIARY
or
INTELLIGENCE SUMMARY
(Erase heading not required.)

Army Form C. 2118.

Instructions regarding War Diaries and Intelligence Summaries are contained in F.S. Regs., Part II. and the Staff Manual respectively. Title Pages will be prepared in manuscript.

Place	Date	Hour	Summary of Events and Information	Remarks and references to Appendices
	Aug 24 (Contd)		Entire Section Hulluch. We have 1 Killed and 2 wounded during the evening.	
TRENCHES	Aug 25/16		A raid is carried out on our left by the 25th Bde, but is unsuccessful. Day quiet. Patrol reconnoitres No Mans land nightly. Capt. Campbell O Coy in asphixt. Battalion Hqrs. at Q.T. AVENUE, off HAY ALLEY. - Col. Paul. Capt. Pakrom. Lieut. Peacock (R.A.M.C).	
	Aug 26/16		Day again very quiet. Grass fatigue have been out during the night, reconnoitring enemy wire and Craters. Wiring parties strengthen our wire in front of O.P.	
	Aug 27/16		Quiet during past twenty four hours.	
	Aug 28/16		Our enemies have been quiet. We are relieved by Border Regt. and Battalion withdraws to PHILOSOPHE when it has in Reserve.	
PHILOSOPHE	Aug 29/16		Baths for Battalion. Headquarters Company is formed: 3 sections: - Hqrs. Section - Under 2nd Lieut. T.W.M. Pakroun. Quartermaster " " " Lieut A.E. Slack. Transport " " " Lieut T.S Pyke-Nott.	

WAR DIARY
or
INTELLIGENCE SUMMARY
(Erase heading not required.)

Army Form C. 2118.

Place	Date	Hour	Summary of Events and Information	Remarks and references to Appendices
PHILOSOPHE	Aug 30.16		Parades under Company arrangements. Weather extremely wet. WMcN	
"	Aug 31.16		Battalion move to Annezin - via BEUVRY - BETHUNE - ANNEZIN. 2nd Platoon move off at 12.30 p.m.; remainder (Platoons at intervals of 200 yards. Brigade in 2nd Divisional Reserve; 11th Border Regt. and 2nd K.O.Y.L.I. in BETHUNE: 16th H.L.I. at BEUVRY.	

W.M. Anderson
Capt. Adjt.
17 H.L.I.

Vol II

Confidential

WAR DIARY. 17th Batt. H.L.I.
from 1st Sept. 1916 till 30th Sept. 1916
Volume II

John R Sandey 2/Lieut-
Intelligence Officer 17/H.L.I.-

Bethune
30 Sept. 1916

Army Form C. 2118.

WAR DIARY
or
INTELLIGENCE SUMMARY

14th Battn. H.L.I.

(Erase heading not required.)

Instructions regarding War Diaries and Intelligence Summaries are contained in F. S. Regs., Part II. and the Staff Manual respectively. Title Pages will be prepared in manuscript.

Place	Date	Hour	Summary of Events and Information	Remarks and references to Appendices
ANNEZIN	Sept 1/16		Parade in forenoon under Company arrangements. Left have gone the battalion. Weather bright and warm. A. Coy. under Capt. Hurman go to School at Parfay.	yes.
"	Sept 2/16		Parade in morning under Coy. arrangements. (Reveille 7 am. breakfast 8 am.)	yes.
"	Sept 3/16		Battalion has baths at BETHUNE.	yes.
"	Sept 4/16		turning wet; but cleared towards 9 am. and the Battalion proceed to the Rifle Range beyond FOUQUEREUIL. Cookers are taken, and dinner is served on the field. Range practices are carried out, and bombing done in the interval.	yes.
"	Sept 5/16		The whole battalion are on trench-fatigue. Busses carry the men from ANNEZIN. The Colonel and Adjutant and Company Officers visit the trenches in the GUINCHY Sector. In the evening is held the Sergeants Anniversary Dinner.	yes.

Army Form C. 2118.

17th Batt. H.L.I.

WAR DIARY
or
INTELLIGENCE SUMMARY
(Erase heading not required.)

Instructions regarding War Diaries and Intelligence Summaries are contained in F. S. Regs., Part II. and the Staff Manual respectively. Title Pages will be prepared in manuscript.

Place	Date	Hour	Summary of Events and Information	Remarks and references to Appendices
ANNEZIN	Sept 6.16		Company training. Weather fine.	JRS
"	Sept 7.16		Company instruction. Intensive of kinds.	JRS
"	Sept 8.16		Battalion relieve 2nd Manchester Regiment in the Cuinchy left subsector; three companies in the firing line B-D-C. A Coy relieve a Coy of Royal Scots in Esperanto Serre. Battalion Head-quarters are in Queen St, at 1st of St Glasgow Road. Relief is carried out quietly, and completed early in the afternoon.	JRS
CUINCHY (left subsector)	Sept 9.16		The past twenty-four hours have been fairly quiet. Intermittent artillery fire on both sides. A lachrymary shell was fired under 2nd Hunts Slee patrolled the Railway Embankment. Capt G R S Pobson. (Adjutant) is awarded the Military Cross for conspicuous gallantry displayed in the battle of July 1st. The award is in immediate recognition. Sergt. J. Ritchie is awarded the Military Medal in immediate recognition of his service on the same date.	JRS
"	Sept 10.16		Good work put in by our T.Ms, Stokes, Vinus, Patata under Capt Howes & Lt. Hon examining	JRS

Army Form 'C. 2118.

WAR DIARY
or
INTELLIGENCE SUMMARY
(Erase heading not required.)

17th Batt- H.L.I.

Place	Date	Hour	Summary of Events and Information	Remarks and references to Appendices
CUINCHY. (Right Subsector)	Sept 11.16.		Quiet day. Patrols again reconnoitred craters at No Mans Land during the night. Enemy fired few rifle grenades, wounding two or eight of our men.	yes
"	Sept 12.16.		Battalion is relieved by 11th Border Regiment and goes into support at Harley St Village km. when it relieves the 2nd K.O.Y.L.I Regiment. Right Kites are garrisoned by now the relief.	yes
CUINCHY.	Sept 13.16.		Battalion in support. Captain Campbell proceeds on course of instruction. Battalion furnish working parties by day & night. Weather good.	yes
"	Sept 14.16.		Still in support. Lt. Lewis wounded by bursting shell in Cuinchy Pat. two draughts of 81 reinforcements arrive at Le Quesnoy, where they are instructed by Cap.t Ralph (Peterson)	yes
"	Sept 15.16.		In support. Continue to feed Kites and furnish working parties.	yes
Left Subsector.	Sept 16.16.		Relieve 11th Border Regiment in left-subsector. Three companies in line. D.C.A.B. Coy in Esperanto Terrace. Day good + relief quietly carried through.	yes
"	Sept 17.16.		2nd Lt Aitchison + T.Mo at 3.15 p.m. carry out a successful shoot on enemy "strong point" at	yes

Army Form C. 2118.

17th Batt. H.L.I.

WAR DIARY
or
INTELLIGENCE SUMMARY
(Erase heading not required.)

Instructions regarding War Diaries and Intelligence Summaries are contained in F. S. Regs., Part II. and the Staff Manual respectively. Title Pages will be prepared in manuscript.

Place	Date	Hour	Summary of Events and Information	Remarks and references to Appendices
COINCHY (left subsector)	Sept 17/16 (cont)	A.16.C.5.5.	Enemy retaliation negligible.	JRA.
	Sept 18/16		Very quiet. Owing to weather observation was impossible. Enemy extra "Rum jar" aerial darts + T.M. on our front rather lively. Our 2" mortars allowed the enemy Patrols under 2nd Lieut Waller + gathered harassing go out during the night.	JRA.
	Sept 19/16		Very quiet day. quiet. Leave resumed. 2nd rest camp stands at Bonbry, num. officer men found to cause of malnutrition at Divisional Relief Station.	JRA.
	Sept 20/16.		Battalion is relieved by 11 Border Regiment during the afternoon, and goes into Brigade Reserve at QUESNOY.	JRA.
"	Sept 21/16.		Baths for Batta at IR Preol. Working parties supplied in large numbers.	JRA.
"	Sept 22/16.		Batta continued to carries. Inspection of latest draught by Commanding Officer.	JRA.
"	Sept 23/16.	Bombing Company Drive	Transport inspected by G. O.C. Commanding Officer proceeded to Boulogne to attend 1st Army School. Battalion left for Brickstacks Sector at 1.30 p.m.	JRA.

Army Form C. 2118.

17th Batt. H.L.I

WAR DIARY
or
INTELLIGENCE SUMMARY

(Erase heading not required.)

Instructions regarding War Diaries and Intelligence Summaries are contained in F. S. Regs., Part II and the Staff Manual respectively. Title Pages will be prepared in manuscript.

Place	Date	Hour	Summary of Events and Information	Remarks and references to Appendices
CUINCHY Left Sub-sector	25.9.16		Line Competition Quiet. Weather fine.	
Bethune.	26.9.16	9 p.m.	A.B.C + D Companies sent out patrols, each consisting of 1 Officer + 12 other ranks, at 9 p.m. Our night + important information was obtained from them. At 3.45 the enemy enemy sent T.M's into our line, during executives at 4 a.m. our Stokes + Newton T.M's opened a heavy bombardment enemy line. The activities on T.M's during the morning from the front line. The 15th Lancashire Fusiliers relieved us commencing at 11 a.m. the battalion then proceeded to billets in BETHUNE	yes yes yes
"	27.9.16		Parades under company arrangements + officers in town	yes
"	28.9.16		Parades under Coy arrangements. 42 men inoculated.	yes
"	29.9.16		Signallers Practice with aeroplane. 70 men inoculated.	yes
"	30.9.16		Practice capturing craters by use of grappling iron ladders (or chevaux)	yes

John Chanley 2/Lt
Intelligence Officer
21/11/HLI

Confidential.

Vol 12

War Diary

(From 1st Oct. 1916 to 31st Oct. 1916)

Vol. III.

John Sanders Lieut
Brevizigus McKim 14th H.L.I
17th N.Z.I.

Army Form C. 2118.

WAR DIARY
or
INTELLIGENCE SUMMARY
(Erase heading not required.)

Instructions regarding War Diaries and Intelligence Summaries are contained in F. S. Regs., Part II and the Staff Manual respectively. Title Pages will be prepared in manuscript.

Place	Date 1916	Hour	Summary of Events and Information	Remarks and references to Appendices
BETHUNE	Oct. 1st		Working parties proceed to trenches in CAMBRIN SECTOR to carry out repairs etc. Leaving billets at 8 a.m. laying wooden lines for ANNEQUIN. They returned at 4 p.m.	yes.
"	2nd		Battalion drill under MAJOR H. MOORE I.S.O. Inoculation.	yes.
"	3rd		Signalling with aeroplane operations postponed owing to weather. Working Party proceeds to trenches in CAMBRIN SECTOR to carry out repairs etc.; other parties under company arrangements.	yes.
Tranchée (MAISON ROUGE) CAMBRIN RIGHT SUBSECTOR	4th		Battalion taken over "village Line" CAMBRIN SECTOR from Manchester Regt. First platoon leaves BETHUNE at 10.30 a.m. Guides were met at ANNEQUIN at 2 p.m. Relief was carried out quietly.	yes.
"	5th		Line very quiet. Numerous fatigues, amounting to 4 Officers + 196 men, supplied.	yes.
"	6th		Line very quiet. In the morning about 12 shells came over new Batt. HQRS. but did no damage. Weather good.	yes.
"	7		Line quiet. Brig. General J.B. JARDINE held a Conference, which C.O's of battalion in 97th Brigade, in Officers mess at MAISON ROUGE.	yes.

WAR DIARY
INTELLIGENCE SUMMARY
(Erase heading not required.)

Army Form C. 2118.

Instructions regarding War Diaries and Intelligence Summaries are contained in F. S. Regs., Part II. and the Staff Manual respectively. Title Pages will be prepared in manuscript.

Place	Date	Hour	Summary of Events and Information	Remarks and references to Appendices
Trenches (Maison Rouge) CAMBRIN RIGHT SECTION Trenches	1916. Oct. 8		Line still very quiet; weather broken. Lines nothing particular.	JCS
"	9		Battalion takes over front line (Boyaux 1-9, CAMBRIN) from 11th BORDER Regt. Relief completed at 4 p.m. (8.10.16). Our T.Ms. bombarded enemy front line at 7.30 p.m. for ½ hour. Two patrols went out in the evening, one under 2/Lieut. CATTO the other under 2/Lieut. MACBETH. Working parties were heard but otherwise everything was very quiet.	JCS
"	10		Our Artillery, T.Ms. & Stokes Guns Active. No retaliation by enemy against Battalion frontage: Lt. Col. W. J. PAUL reported Battalion; Two patrols on under 2/Lieut. T. CATTO, and the other under 2/Lieut. DUNSMUIR went out from our lines to examine enemy wire.	JCS
"	11		Our T.Ms. and Stokes Guns bombarded enemy line all along our frontage from 4 p.m. to 5 p.m. (10.10.16) Enemy retaliation about one dozen heavy T.Ms. At 1.30 a.m. (11-10-16) enemy patrol coming from A 28. C. 9. 2 dispersed by Lewis Gunfire. Two patrols went out from our line but owing to bright moonlight and lack of cover were unable to accomplish much.	JCS

Army Form C. 2118.

WAR DIARY
or
INTELLIGENCE SUMMARY
(Erase heading not required.)

Instructions regarding War Diaries and Intelligence Summaries are contained in F. S. Regs, Part II. and the Staff Manual respectively. Title Pages will be prepared in manuscript.

Place	Date	Hour	Summary of Events and Information	Remarks and references to Appendices
Trenches TAMBOUR RIGHT SUBSECTION	1916 12 Oct.		A patrol, consisting of 2nd Lieut. Batts & two O.R. left Sally Port at A.28.c.7.4 to reconnoitre enemy sap opposite. Found sap had lately changed by our T.M. fire. No signs of wire round sap. Trench working parties. Artillery co-operated in T.M. bombardment of enemy line between 3 & 4 p.m. (11-10-16). Enemy replied with "whizz-bangs" - searches for our heavy T.M's with 5.9's.	JCS
"	13 Oct.		With the exception of Artillery and T.M. activity, everything was quiet.	JCS
"	14 Oct.		Relieved today by 10th K.O.Y.L.I. (21st Division). Guards out guarding and completed by 1 p.m. 14-10-16. Trek over visible in Beaury.	JCS
Beaury	15 Oct.		Left Beaury at 9.30 a.m. and proceeded to Lahoumière via Beaume. Destination reached at 11.45 a.m. taken over shortly afterwards.	JCS
Lahoumière	16 Oct.		Church Parade at 2 p.m. yesterday followed by company drill. Left Lahoumière at 7 a.m. 16-10-16 and proceeded to La Thienloye via Division and Busten. Arrived at 1 p.m. Trek over thick.	JCS
La Thienloye	17 Oct.		Battalion left for "Mantle en Yemen" at 6.45 a.m. arriving about 11.30 a.m. which on outpost scheme was carried out.	JCS
Mantle en Yemen	18 Oct.		Battalion left for "Hardinval" at 4 a.m. + arrived there at 1 p.m.	JCS
Hardinval	19 Oct.		Battalion left for RUBEMPRE at 7.30 a.m. On arriving at a point about + many orders were received to return to "HARDINVAL". Very wet day.	JCS

WAR DIARY
INTELLIGENCE SUMMARY
(Erase heading not required.)

Army Form C. 2118.

Instructions regarding War Diaries and Intelligence Summaries are contained in F.S. Regs., Part II and the Staff Manual respectively. Title Pages will be prepared in manuscript.

Place	Date	Hour	Summary of Events and Information	Remarks and references to Appendices
Houchinpré	20 Oct.		Today spent in parades under Company arrangements. Bombing, throwing again any. Drafts of 52 r. & f. joined Battalion.	JCB
"	21 Oct.		Battalion left for Rubempré at 7.30 a.m. and arrived there at 12.45 p.m. Took over Billets.	JCB
Rubempré	22 Oct.		Battalion Drill this morning under Major Morton; immediate return of men issued from G.O.C. 32nd Division to S.M. Morton and Quarter master Sgt. Brenman for their devotion to duty and gallantry in the fires. Ammunition returns followed by Communion Service.	JCB
"	23 "		Inf. Rubempré at 11 a.m. and proceeded by way of Hérissart, Contay, and Miriancourt to Bouzincourt. Arrived at 6.45 & 10th over Billets.	JCB
Bouzincourt	24 "		Barrage fire Drill in Companies this forenoon. Party of Officers and senior N.C.O.'s went over ground between Bouzincourt towards Ovillers. Infantry tracks obliterated & difficult to follow. Weather very wet.	JCB
"	25.		Weather still very wet. Inspection of gas helmets during forenoon.	JCB
"	26		Battle order inspection by Companies this forenoon. Fatigue parties supplied. Artillery formation tactics carried out by Battalion during afternoon. On this parade it was intimated that the following award had been made to the Battalion by G.O.C. 10th Army Corps for	JCB

WAR DIARY
or
INTELLIGENCE SUMMARY

Army Form C. 2118.

(Erase heading not required.)

Place	Date	Hour	Summary of Events and Information	Remarks and references to Appendices
Bouzincourt	26 Oct.	cont'd.	gallantry in the first during the operations on 1st July, 1916. Subsequent dates :- (1) No 15748 Sergt. J. McGregor: 156770 Sergt. Joseph Maynee: (3) 16048 Sergt. Piper Young Gillard: (4) 15419 Corpl. (now Sergt.) D. M. Reid: (5) 15956 Sergt. William Glenward: (6) Corpl. John Roberts: (7) 15964 Sergt. John Osborne: Sergt. McGregor: Sergt. Glenward: Piper Gillard received Ribbons on parade.	JRS
"	27) "		Large fatigue parties supplied by Battalion for work in trenches. Weather still very inclement.	JRS
"	28 "		Advancing in Artillery formation & Barrage fire Drill by Battalion. Large fatigue parties supplied for work in trenches.	JRS
"	29 "		Large fatigue parties supplied for work in trenches.	JRS
"	30 "		Left Bouzincourt at 8.30 a.m. and proceeded via Senlis, Harley, Contay and Hérissart to RUBEMPRÉ. Arrived at 1.30 p.m. and took over billets. Fair inspections.	JRS
Rubempré	31 "	Gen.	Left Rubempré at 10.45 a.m., destination CANAPLES, route via Talmas & Naours. Turned on outskirts of latter village on intelligence that there was no billeting accommodation at Canaples. Returned to emergency camps at VAL'. DE. MAISON. Arrived 2.30 p.m. Weather improved.	JRS

John R Danley 2nd Lieut.
Intelligence Officer 17th H.L.I.

Confidential

91/32
Vol 13

WAR DIARY.

1st to 30th November, 1916 (inclusive).

Volume 12.

17th H.L.I.

D.G. Thorburn
2Lt

WAR DIARY
or
INTELLIGENCE SUMMARY

(Erase heading not required.)

Army Form C. 2118.

Place	Date	Hour	Summary of Events and Information	Remarks and references to Appendices
VAL-DE-MAISON	1916 Nov. 1st		Still under canvas; weather inclement; parades under Company arrangements – Bayonet fighting; practice bombing; physical drill to Battalion. Drill in afternoon.	D.G.7.
"	2		Morning wet. Battalion took part in Brigade Scheme – an attack on La Vicogne. Rendez-vous small wood in centre of triangle Val de Maison, Wainneville and Rubempré; zero time 2.20 p.m. Attack finished at 6.20 p.m. Batt. transport returned to Val de Maison; reached us 7 p.m.	D.G.7.
"	3		Morning wet. Parades under Company arrangements. Bombing, close order drill, P.T.	D.G.7.
"	4		Still under canvas. Bombing, physical close order drill under Company arrangements in forenoon. Battalion drill in afternoon.	D.G.7.
"	5		Weather very stormy. Church Parade in forenoon followed by Lecture by Lieut. Sharratt (Divisional Gas School) on protection against enemy Gas shells.	D.G.7.
"	6		Battalion took part today in a Brigade Scheme. Attack beyond Ferme du Roust in direction of Beauval. Left camp at 8.45 a.m.; returned 3 p.m.	D.G.Y.
"	7		Company parades in tents owing to very inclement weather; kit inspections.	D.G.7.
"	8		Weather very wet during forenoon. Short route march in afternoon via Puchevillers. Left camp 2 p.m. returned 4.15 p.m.	D.G.7.
"	9		Parades under Company arrangements in forenoon & afternoon.	D.G.7.
"	10		Parades under Company arrangements in forenoon. Short route march in afternoon.	D.G.7.

WAR DIARY
or
INTELLIGENCE SUMMARY
(Erase heading not required.)

Army Form C. 2118.

Place	Date	Hour	Summary of Events and Information	Remarks and references to Appendices
VAL-DE-MAISON	11th Nov.		Parades under Company arrangements; training.	D.9.7
"	12 "		Church Parade this forenoon, followed by Battalion drill by Lt. Col. N. J. Paul.	D.9.7
"	13 "		Left Val-de-Maison at 11.15 a.m. Proceeded via Hérissart, Mirvaux to Vadencourt Wood. Arrived 3.30 p.m. Took over huttments.	D.9.7
VADENCOURT.	14 "		Parades under Company arrangements in forenoon; Inspections. Left Vadencourt Wood at 1 p.m. Proceeded by way of Warloy, Senlis, Bouzincourt, Aveluy to Martinsart Valley. Arriving 5.15 p.m. Took over huttments.	D.9.7
Martinsart Valley.	15 "		Orders to prepare to go into action; arrangements made to and detail to not going into action to Bouzincourt; again, orders to proceed to Englebelmer, fore-marching orders. Proceeded there via Martinsart, arriving 4.45 p.m. Took over trenches.	D.9.7
ENGLEBELMER	16 "		System of trenches opposite Beaumont-Hamel visited by C.O. this forenoon. Order to prepare to go into action and Beaumont dumpsfret; packs and Blankets drawn and night spent in trenches.	D.9.7
"	17 "		C.O. and Company Commanders re-visited system of trenches this forenoon. Order to prepare to go into action and arrangements made accordingly. Details of such men left in Englebelmer. Battalion left trench at 2 p.m. and proceeded via Mailly Mailet to Auchonvillers Station where guides of the 4th Seaforths were met.	D.9.7

Army Form C. 2118.

WAR DIARY
or
INTELLIGENCE SUMMARY
(Erase heading not required.)

1st M.C.

Instructions regarding War Diaries and Intelligence Summaries are contained in F. S. Regs., Part II and the Staff Manual respectively. Title Pages will be prepared in manuscript.

Place	Date	Hour	Summary of Events and Information	Remarks and references to Appendices
Beaumont Hamel.	Nov. 17. (contd.)		Relief commenced at once and completed by 7 p.m. Intermittent shelling. At 10 p.m. our casualties 2 o.r. wounded.	D97.
"	" 18		Arrangements for artillery barrage and programme of artillery fire sent to Company Commanders early this morning. Snow commenced to fall in the early hours, later turning to rain. 7 cold & wet. At 4.40 a.m. message sent to Company Commanders that Zero time is 6.10 a.m.	D97.
		6.10 a.m.	Clouds commenced at 6.10 a.m. Held up owing to insufficiency of our artillery barrage. Heavy enemy machine gun fire.	
		7.42 a.m.	Message from right company that company commander is wounded and that a Sergeant and about 10 men holding right flank. M.G. officer attached reports that attack seems to be held up. Fine. Later officer ordered to take back two guns in New Munich Trench.	D97.
		7.50 a.m.	Message sent to B. Company to relieve if possible from no Mans Land and reoccupy New Munich Trench. Messenger from right company reports that O.C. company is killed and only one officer left, so far as is known; that latter officer and a few men are lying out in front of New Munich Trench.	D97.

WAR DIARY
or
INTELLIGENCE SUMMARY

(Erase heading not required.)

Army Form C. 2118.

Place	Date	Hour	Summary of Events and Information	Remarks and references to Appendices
	Nov. 1916	contd		
		8.10 a.m.	Estimated casualties:- 2 Captains; 10 Subalterns; 330 other ranks.	
		8.30 a.m.	Following message received from 2nd Lieut. MACBETH of night company. "Am holding old front line with remainder of Battalion" "and have established a bombing post on the right." "There are only Lieut. MARTIN and myself in the trench." Enemy shelling ground in front of New Munich Trench and enemy snipers very active. New Munich Trench now held by 2 officers and about 50 men. Unwounded men continuing to come in slowly from No Man's Land.	D.9.7.
		9.18 a.m.	H.Q. Officer sent to reorganise, reports as follows:- "Line held by 4 vickers guns; 3 Lewis guns, 2 officers" "and a little over 100 men; enemy still shelling" "slightly."	
		10 a.m.	Following message from Lieut. Dobson, commanding left centre company:- "Am at present in shell hole with 5 unwounded and" "one badly wounded man. I am slightly hit and" "intend"	D.9.7

WAR DIARY
or
INTELLIGENCE SUMMARY

Army Form **2118**.

Place	Date	Hour	Summary of Events and Information	Remarks and references to Appendices
	18th Nov. 1916 contd:-		"intend waiting two with a Corporal till after dark, when we shall endeavour to bring in Private Bruce, badly wounded."	DGT.
		10.35 am	Total number of Officers, N.C.O's and men now in New Munich Trench – 101.	
		11 am	Following unaccounted for:- 2nd Lieuts R. Stewart; F.R. Jones; A. Dewar; F.C. Steele; A.R. Murray; A.F. Roberts; T. Neilson, and C.J. Macewan, and 340 other ranks. 2nd Lieut. Martin reports as follows:- "When barrage opened, a great number of shells fell just in front of New Munich Trench where our companies were lying out, killing and wounding a large number of men. When barrage lifted on to Munich Trench for last four minutes, it was still short and when the leading waves came up to about 50 or 60 yards from Munich Trench, following up the barrage, I saw the Germans lying in the Trench in force." "do	DGT.

WAR DIARY
or
INTELLIGENCE SUMMARY

(Erase heading not required.)

Army Form C. 2118.

Place	Date	Hour	Summary of Events and Information	Remarks and references to Appendices
	18th Nov. 1916.	Cont'd	"So soon as 9 to the trench, that I opened fire with my machine; then the barrage was on Munich Trench" "for 4 minutes, the enemy's machine guns flared on" "us from lock flanks all the time." "The failure of the attack was due, in my "opinion to :—" " (1) The utter insufficiency of our barrage." " (2) The condition of the ground, — there having been" " in and rain falling on the snow making" " it slipping." " (3) The extreme cold which prevailed."	D9.7.
		2.45 p.m.	Message sent that our guns are firing on New Munich Trench and Leave Alley and asking to correct range immediately. Brigade informed that in the event of the enemy counter attacking, resistance could not be very prolonged.	
		10.45 p.m.	Relieved	

WAR DIARY
or
INTELLIGENCE SUMMARY
(Erase heading not required.)

Army Form C. 2118.

Place	Date	Hour	Summary of Events and Information	Remarks and references to Appendices
	18th Nov. 1916.	cont.d 10.45 p.m.	Casualty return:— Killed:— Capt. J.S. MARR; 2nd Lieuts. A.F. ROBERTS & C.J. MACEWAN Died of Wounds:— Capt. J.F. MORRISON. Wounded:— 2nd Lieuts. J.W.M. PATERSON & R. STEWART. Slightly Wounded:— Lieut. E. DOBSON and R.A. DRYSDALE. (on duty) Unaccounted for:— 2nd Lieuts. F.R. JONES; R. DEWAR; F.G. STEELE; A.R. MURRAY; T. NEILSON. Killed, wounded & missing:— 300 other ranks.	
		11.35 p.m.	Situation report as follows:— "Artillery fire on both sides continues. Clearing of No Mans Land and evacuation of wounded continues."	D97.
	19th Nov. 1916.	1 a.m.	Relief commenced by 15th LANC. FUS. Completed at 6 a.m. Battalion returned to Mailly-Maillet and took over billets there. Remainder of day spent resting.	D97.

WAR DIARY or INTELLIGENCE SUMMARY

Army Form C. 2118.

14th H.L.I.

Place	Date	Hour	Summary of Events and Information	Remarks and references to Appendices
MAILLY-MAILLET	1916. 20 Nov.		Today spent cleaning equipment, refitting and taking final casualty return :- Killed and missing - 63 o.r.; Wounded 143 o.r.; officers 9 killed; 2 wounded; a slightly wounded (on duty). Carrying parties returned to trenches tonight to bring down wounded men of the 17th who had been left in a dug-out that this day-out having been used as an Advanced aid post during the attack. Parties returned to Mailly at 6.15 a.m.	D97.
"	21 Nov.		Brigade inspected this forenoon by G.O.C. 5th Army. Fatigue party of 50 men proceeded to trenches.	D97.
"	22 "		Parades under company arrangements; inspections and incidents; parade of officers and senior N.C.O.'s to arrange new marching order for equipment in view of probable move tomorrow.	D97.
"	23 "		Battalion left MAILLY-MAILLET today at 12.25 pm and proceeded via Hédauville, Varennes, Leaheux, & Argoeuves to Rainchéval, arriving at 5 pm. Took our billets there.	D97.
"	24 "		Parades under company arrangements: large road working party supplied by Battalion.	D97.
RAINCHEVAL	25 "		Left Rainchéval at 9.20 am. Proceeded via Beauquesne, Terramesnil, & Hurieux to BEAUVAL arrived 12.30. Took over billets. Weather very wet.	D97.

Army Form C. 2118.

WAR DIARY
or
INTELLIGENCE SUMMARY
(Erase heading not required.)

17th A/Q

Instructions regarding War Diaries and Intelligence Summaries are contained in F. S. Regs., Part II. and the Staff Manual respectively. Title Pages will be prepared in manuscript.

Place	Date 1916	Hour	Summary of Events and Information	Remarks and references to Appendices
BEAUVAL	26/Nov.		Left Beauval at 9.15 a.m. & proceeded via Candas, Fienvillers, Bernevil to Domart-en-Ponthieu. Billets being unobtainable in this village proceeded to Franqueville. Arrived at 2.30 p.m. Took over billets.	D.G.T.
FRANQUEVILLE	27 "		Parades under company arrangements: forenoon inspections & close order drill: afternoon spent cleaning up & reconnoitring billets.	D.G.T.
"	28 "		Bathing at Divisional Baths in Domart this forenoon. Parades under Company arrangements.	D.G.T.
"	29 "		Parades under company arrangements; physical & close order drill; musketry course for men "F.O." commenced under 2/Lieut Fairweather.	D.G.T.
"	30 "		Parades under Company arrangements; physical drill; close order drill; bombing, &c.	D.G.T.

Douglas G. Thorburn
Lt.
17th H.L.I.

2/12/16.

Vol 14

17th Service Battalion
Highland Light Infantry

Confidential.

War Diary.

1st December 1916 — 31st Decr 1916

Jas. Bracelin Lieut

Volume 4 Number 4

WAR DIARY or INTELLIGENCE SUMMARY

(Erase heading not required.)

Army Form C. 2118.

Place	Date	Hour	Summary of Events and Information	Remarks and references to Appendices
FRANQUE-VILLE	1916. 1st Dec.		Parades by companies today as per programme made up & approved by Brigade; Physical relax. order drill; bombing; gas helmet drill.	ASB
"	2 "		Parades as per programme; Physical relax. order drill bombing; bayonet fighting in morning.	ASB.
"	3 "		Church Parade in forenoon; Service conducted by 2nd Lieut. Smith.	ASB.
"	4 "		Games in afternoon as per programme; Inoculations.	ASB.
"	5 "		Route marches by companies in forenoon. Games in afternoon as per programme. T.A.B. inoculations.	ASB.
"	6 "		Parades by companies as per programme; 4 cases enteric pro-gramme.	ASB.
"	7 "		Parades by companies as per programme. B. coy. on Bayonet. Fighting; Afternoon games as per programme.	ASB.
"	8 "		Morning run. Parades by companies as per programme. C. Coy. on Bayonet Fighting Ground; Afternoon; games as per programme. Inclement weather; inspection by Companies in billets; free marching order; games in afternoon as per programme.	ASB.
"	9 "		2 men of 32 r.T. join Battalion. Parades by companies as per programme; A Coy. on the range; teams in afternoon football owing to wet weather. Further drafts of 50 r.T. joins Battalion today.	ASB.

2449 Wt. W14957/M90 750,000 1/16 J.B.C. & A. Forms/C.2118/12.

Army Form C. 2118.

WAR DIARY
or
INTELLIGENCE SUMMARY
(Erase heading not required.)

Place	Date	Hour	Summary of Events and Information	Remarks and references to Appendices
FRANQUEVILLE	1916. 10 Dec.		Preliminary Inspection parade this forenoon. No games in afternoon owing to inclement weather.	
"	11 "	"	Battalion inspected this forenoon by G.O.C. 5th Army Corps. Games in afternoon as per programme.	A813.
"	12 "	"	Weather very inclement; no parade; no games in forenoon. Tactical exercises for Officers in afternoon; no games. Excerpts from Part II Orders of date :-	A813.
			"The following Extract from the "London Gazette", dated 25th Nov. 1916, is published for information :- "His Majesty the King has been graciously pleased " to confer the Victoria Cross on the under- "mentioned Officers, Non-commissioned Officers and " men.	
			No. 15,888. Sergeant JAMES YOUNG TURNBULL, late Highland Light Infantry.	

WAR DIARY or INTELLIGENCE SUMMARY

Army Form C. 2118.

Place	Date	Hour	Summary of Events and Information	Remarks and references to Appendices
FRANQUE-VILLE	1916 12 Decr.	contd.	"for most conspicuous bravery and devotion to duty. "Having with his party captured a post apparently "of great importance to the enemy, he was sub- "jected to severe counter-attacks which were "continuous throughout the day. Although "his party was wiped out and replaced several "times during the day Sergeant Turnbull never "wavered in his determination to hold the post "the loss of which would have been very serious. "Almost single-handed, he maintained his "position and displayed the highest degree of "valour and skill in the performance of his "duties." "Later in the day this very gallant soldier "was killed whilst bombing a counter-attack "from the parados of our trench."	AST3

WAR DIARY or **INTELLIGENCE SUMMARY**

Army Form C. 2118.

Place	Date	Hour	Summary of Events and Information	Remarks and references to Appendices
FRANQUEVILLE	1916 13 Decr.		Battalion proceeded to BARLETTE to carry out exercises in communication between infantry and contact aeroplane. Exercises postponed owning to low visibility. Battalion continued en Route march via Rubempré & Toutencourt. Returned about 12.30 p.m. Afternoon Games; B. Company on range.	JSB.
"	14 Decr.		Bombing competition by companies; 'C' Coy. on range; selected Officers & N.C.O.'s receive instruction in Bayonet fighting. Games in afternoon.	JSB.
"	15 "		Parades by companies in billets owing to inclement weather; D. Coy. had use of range.	JSB.
"	16 "		Battalion left Franqueville at 10.30 a.m. and proceeded via Donart-en-Ponthieu & St Léger to Berteaucourt — arrived at 12.20 p.m. and took over billets. Draft of 100 N. & B. joined Battalion next; also two officers	JSB.
Berteaucourt	17 "		Battalion left Berteaucourt at 8 a.m. & proceeded via Halloy-en-Pernois, Bonaféa, Havernas, Harpnes, Naours and Talmas to Rubempré arriving 1.30 p.m. took over billets.	JSB.
Rubempré	18 "		Fatigues and C.O. inspection of Battalion in morning; games in afternoon as per programme orders in forenoon.	JSB.

Army Form C. 2118.

WAR DIARY
or
INTELLIGENCE SUMMARY
(Erase heading not required.)

Instructions regarding War Diaries and Intelligence Summaries are contained in F. S. Regs., Part II. and the Staff Manual respectively. Title Pages will be prepared in manuscript.

Place	Date	Hour	Summary of Events and Information	Remarks and references to Appendices
Rubempre	19th Decr		Company parade as assigned in scheme of training. Inspection by Army Commander arranged for the afternoon did not take place	
	20th	"	Company parades as assigned in scheme of training in the forenoon. Games in the afternoon. 17th Bn Highland L.I. won Brigade Football Championship being 2nd Bn K.O.Y.L.I. in the final by 4 goals to 1.	
	21st	"	Company parades as assigned in scheme of training. Staff of 9 men and 2 officers arrived for the Battn. Games in the afternoon	
	22nd	"	Brigade march arranged for forenoon cancelled on account of inclement weather. Inspection of kits by Coy Commanders and lectures in billets instead. Games in the afternoon - Rugby match C Coy versus Rest of Battn.	
	23rd	"	Company training as assigned in scheme of training. Fitting of Box Respirators. Brigade Bayonet Fighting Competition at Pucheviller in the forenoon. Games in the afternoon	
	24th	"	Battn. Church parade and inspection of billets and kits by the C.O. in the forenoon. 17th Bn Highland L.I. beat 16 Bn Highland L.I. in the forenoon 2 by 3 goals Games in the afternoon. to 0	

Army Form C. 2118.

WAR DIARY
or
INTELLIGENCE SUMMARY
(Erase heading not required.)

Instructions regarding War Diaries and Intelligence Summaries are contained in F. S. Regs., Part II and the Staff Manual respectively. Title Pages will be prepared in manuscript.

Place	Date	Hour	Summary of Events and Information	Remarks and references to Appendices
Rulempsi	25th Dec.		Christmas day:- no parade. Games:- in the forenoon the officers beat the Sergeants at Rugby by 11 points to 0 :- in the afternoon "B" Coy beat H.Qrs Coy by 4 goals to nil in the final of the Batt Championship :- in the evening a very successful Battn concert was held.	JSB
	26th Dec.		Brigade route march via Le Val de Maison, Beauquesne, Puchevillers, back to Rulempsi. Inspection of feet in the afternoon.	JSB
	27th Dec.		Reorganization of companies and Platoons in the forenoon. Lecture in the afternoon to officers and N.C.O's on "trench feet". Team from the 17th Batt. H.L.I. won the Brigade Cross Country race at 7 miles.	JSB
	28th Dec.		Company parades as assigned in scheme of training and fatigues. Football matches arranged for the afternoon cancelled. The Batt Rugby match v. 11th Border Regiment on account of frost. B Coy v. Divisional artillery because "B" Coy were on duty. Practice Cross-Country run in the afternoon. Captain W.W. Morton relinquishes his Acting Rank of Major on ceasing to be employed as 2nd in Command of the Battalion, with effect from 11-12-1916.	JSB

WAR DIARY or INTELLIGENCE SUMMARY

Army Form C. 2118.

Place	Date	Hour	Summary of Events and Information	Remarks and references to Appendices
Richeupe	29th Dec		Company parades as assigned in scheme of training and working parties. Lecture at 6 p.m. to officers on Horsemanship and care of horses. Practice cross-country run in the afternoon. Xmas dinners and entertainments given to A and B Coys in the evening.	JSB
	30th Dec		Company parades and working parties. In the afternoon the Batt. team beat the 3/6 Batt. Royal Scots in the semi-final of the Divisional Football Competition by 2 goals to nil. In the evening Xmas dinners and entertainments were given to C, D, and HQ.rs Coys. A special inspection of the transport and the Company cookers by the Commanding officer in the afternoon.	JSB.
	31st Dec		Church parade in the morning. Undermentioned N.C.O.'s and men presented with the Military Medal by the General Commanding the 5th Army Corps. 2984 Sgt N. Connor "B" Coy 15938 Sgt A.G. Watson "C" Coy 15581 Pte C.N. Fraser "C" Coy 13699 " R.J. Slowey "D" Coy 43268 " J. Scott "B" Coy In the final of the Divisional Cross Country run the 17th Batt.H.L.I were beaten by the 2nd Batt Dorset Regiment. Batt Rugby team beat the Machine Gun Coy by 36 points to nil. Batt concert in the evening.	JSB.

WAR DIARY or INTELLIGENCE SUMMARY

Army Form C. 2118.

17. A.Z.1. Vol 15
January 1917

Place	Date	Hour	Summary of Events and Information	Remarks and references to Appendices
RUBEMPRE	Jany/1. 1917		Tactical exercise carried out in conjunction with the 16th 13 Batt. H.L.I. In the afternoon the Batt Team won the Divisional Football Championship beating the 2nd Batt Enniskillen Fusiliers in the final by 4 goals to 3. The bayonet fighting team took part in the Brigade Competition. Col. Paul resumed command of the Batt on his return from leave. The Batt. is ordered to hold itself in readiness to move up to the line.	A&D/
"	2		Parades today under Company arrangements: combined bayonet fighting, i.e. C.O. and company Commanders visited trenches today.	A&D/
"	3		Large fatigue parties supplied by Battalion today for work at Puchevillers. Remainder of Battalion paraded under Company arrangements.	A&D/
"	4		Battalion paraded at 7:10 a.m. and proceeded beyond Puchevillers where tactical exercises were carried out in conjunction with 16th Batt. H.L.I. Weather extremely wet. Afternoon parades cancelled. Foot inspections in billets. Working parties supplied for work on range.	A&D/
"	5		Bathing at Puchevillers. Parades made by Companies as per Batt. Orders of 4th inst, see 4.	

Army Form C. 2118.

WAR DIARY
or
INTELLIGENCE SUMMARY
(Erase heading not required.)

Place	Date	Hour	Summary of Events and Information	Remarks and references to Appendices
Courcelles	1917 Jany 6.		Left Rubempré at 7.30 a.m. and proceeded by motor lorries to Bus-en-Artois and thence in column of route to Courcelles where we billeted. Arrived 11.30 a.m. Following additional honours have been announced to the Battalion:- Military Crosses to Captains Russell and Drysdale and C.S.M. Dunsmuir. D.C.M. to Sergt J. Zeiper.	App.
"	"	7	Battalion goes into the trenches - out-sector C.3, relieving troops of the 3rd Division. Relief commenced at 5 p.m.; completed at 8.10 p.m. Night quiet except for intermittent shelling. A.B. & C. Coys in line. D. Coy in support.	App.
Trenches	"	8	Patrol left our line at 11.30 p.m. (7.1.17) to examine wire in front of our out-post line between Benown & Southern Trenches; wire good but in parts requires strengthening. Patrol returned 12.30 a.m. Enemy shelling N. of Rot Roy & Monk Trenches between 6.45 a.m. & 7.15 a.m. Enemy T.M.s active against Rot. Roy. Heavy rain during night. Trenches in a bad state. Pumping being carried on. Our artillery very active in afternoon against enemy trenches.	App.
"	"	9	Weather still bad. Pumping going on. Patrol examined wire between N° 3 and N° 4 posts - found a good obstacle. Artillery bombardment of enemy lines opposite Batt. frontage started at 8 a.m. today & has continued throughout the day with varying intensity, good shooting was observed. Enemy re- plied slightly against Rot. Roy and Monk Trenches. Enemy's reply weak.	App.

WAR DIARY
or
INTELLIGENCE SUMMARY

(Erase heading not required.)

Army Form C. 2118.

Place	Date	Hour	Summary of Events and Information	Remarks and references to Appendices
Trenches	1917. 10 Jany.		Bad weather continues; pumping going on; The night was quiet on our frontage. Artillery again subjected the enemy trenches to a severe bombardment, which continued throughout the whole day. The T.M's co-operated in the afternoon. The enemy's retaliation was more than usual, being extremely heavy at the time of the change over. The relief was, in consequence, delayed. On relief, Battalion proceeded to Courcelles and 10th Div. Res. Bns. Our casualties during this spell were 5 O.R. wounded. 7 Officers joined Batt. yesty. Draft of 11 O.R. joined Battalion.	Appx A (?)
Courcelles	11 Jany.		Today spent in cleaning up, foot inspections up, kit inspections r.e. Party carrying for rations and water tring supplies tonight.	Appx B
"	12 "		Today spent in preparation for going into the line. Gum boots have been issued to all ranks. Each man carries at least three pairs of socks. Rubbing of feet with whale oil is being done frequently. Took over trenches in Sub-Sector C.3 from 11th Border Regt. Relief completed at 12.50 a.m.	Appx B

WAR DIARY or INTELLIGENCE SUMMARY

Army Form C. 2118.

Place	Date	Hour	Summary of Events and Information	Remarks and references to Appendices
Trenches	1917. 13 Jany.		Night relatively quiet. At 11 a.m. enemy put up a barrage with 77 m.m. shells on Rue Roy and Mantz Trenches, the support trenches being at the same time shelled with 5.9". Artillery retaliation was asked for but given. During the forenoon, the enemy's artillery was particularly active against our trenches south of Matthews Copse and in K. 29. C. Situation normal during the afternoon. Slight artillery activity on our part towards evening. Sleet has fallen all day & conditions are very bad. Pumping of trenches continues.	App 16(a)
"	14 "		Night calm on the whole. About 5 a.m. enemy's artillery shelled our trenches with more than average intermittency. Our artillery was asked for retaliation. Trench fire was kept up on enemy trenches for five minutes at 5.30 am. repeated at 5.50. Enemy shelling was very mighty heavy trenches at times heavily made from support lines. Relief commenced by 16th Lancs. Fus. at 6 p.m. Late in evening Col. n. cm. p. s. Rct. and artillery emplacements shelled with tear shell.	App 16(b)
"	15 "		Relief completed in the early hours of this morning. Day spent in dressing, cleaning up, & for inspections. Rifle inspection twice parties supplied.	App 16(c)

Army Form C. 2118.

WAR DIARY
or
INTELLIGENCE SUMMARY
(Erase heading not required.)

Instructions regarding War Diaries and Intelligence Summaries are contained in F. S. Regs., Part II. and the Staff Manual respectively. Title Pages will be prepared in manuscript.

Place	Date	Hour	Summary of Events and Information	Remarks and references to Appendices
BUS	1917. 16 Jany.		Large fatigue parties have been supplied today by the Battalion for work on roads, &c. Weather cold with heavy snowfall. Draft of 7 o.r. joined Battalion today.	M(3)
"	17	"	Fatigue parties supplied by Battalion. Works &c &c's & changes continue. Rifle inspections &c.	M(3)
"	18	"	Fatigue parties supplied by Battalion. Battalion concert tonight.	M(3)
"	19	"	Fatigue parties supplied by Battalion. Rifle Inspections etc	M(3)
"	20	"	17th Bn. H.L.I. relieved the 9th Devons in Brigade Reserve in BEAUMONT-HAMEL. Two Companies in the BURN. Two Companies in B.14.a.8.8. Relief took place in afternoon. Weather beginning of hard frost. Work.	M(6)
TRENCHES	21	"	Weather - Hard frost and sunshine. Battalion supplied fatigues to R.E. & Officers and 195 other ranks.	M(6)
"	22	"	Weather. Severe frost and snow, low visibility. Coy Commanders meeting at 10.30 A.M. Fatigues supplied for carrying Lewis & Gun Stocks.	M(6)

Army Form C. 2118.

WAR DIARY
or
INTELLIGENCE SUMMARY

(Erase heading not required.)

Instructions regarding War Diaries and Intelligence Summaries are contained in F. S. Regs., Part II and the Staff Manual respectively. Title Pages will be prepared in manuscript.

Place	Date	Hour	Summary of Events and Information	Remarks and references to Appendices
TRENCHES	23 Jany		A and D Companies and Half Battalion Headquarters relieved 11th BORDER REGIMENT in R.1 Sub sector. Half Battalion Headquarters was at STATION ROAD. B & C Companies stayed in O.14.a.8.8. in supports and furnished fatigue parties as follows:- 3 Officers and 150 other ranks for AUCHONVILLERS and 2 Officers and 50 other ranks for MAILLY MAILLET. VICTORY Post established.	M&D
"	24 "		POLLS PERCH established. Lewis was lying to these posts. Patrols were out in R.1.a. and encountered hostile patrols who were challenged and answered 11-5 11th Coy 3rd Bavarian R.I.R.	M&D
"	25 "		B & C Coys relieved A & D Coys in R.1. Subsector. Patrols encountered a hostile patrol on ridge in R.1.a.	M&D
"	26 "		A hostile patrol left VICTORY POST to attack hostile post situated in R.1.a. Artillery Barrage for 10 minutes during which patrol crept out and not the position. This post was carried but no enemy were in garrison. There were signs of enemy tracks in vicinity. 300 Counts of Enquiry	M&D

WAR DIARY
or
INTELLIGENCE SUMMARY

Army Form C. 2118.

Place	Date	Hour	Summary of Events and Information	Remarks and references to Appendices
TRENCHES	27 Jany		B & C Coys 14th H.L.I. were relieved by two Coys 16th H.L.I. the whole Battalion withdrew to Brigade in BEAUMONT-HAMEL in Brigade Reserve. Working parties of 200 yards were found each night to work in Artillery Lines. Three men wounded in R.E. fatigue.	(M.9)
"	28 "		A Defence of BEAUMONT-HAMEL was drawn up as follows STUARTS, CAMPBELLS, HARPERS, HAMILTON, and BORN WORK. Statues were found during the night as usual.	(K.9)
"	29 "		1/2 Battalion relieved Coys 11th BORDER REGIMENT in R.2. Sub-sector. A & D Coys in front line, and B & C Coys in support. Patrols Report.— Enemy posts near WAGGON ROAD close to TENTREE ALLEY.	(3K)
"	30 "		Artillery carried out shoots on K36d at 4.45 & 8.45 p.m. Also on CR.1.a at 12 midnight. Various parties of Enemy were seen during the day.	(K.9)

Army Form C. 2118.

WAR DIARY
or
INTELLIGENCE SUMMARY

(Erase heading not required.)

Instructions regarding War Diaries and Intelligence Summaries are contained in F. S. Regs., Part II and the Staff Manual respectively. Title Pages will be prepared in manuscript.

Place	Date	Hour	Summary of Events and Information	Remarks and references to Appendices
TRENCHES	31 Jany		At 5.30am enemy carried out a hurricane bombardment with trench mortars on our left Coy front. First appearance of Mortars. Artillery carried out desultory fire on same during the day.	M&P

SECRET

14.NL/.

No. 16

CONFIDENTIAL

WAR DIARY.

From 1st February to 28th February 1914.—

W.K. Oakley Capt
GSO for 2nd Lieut.
INTELLIGENCE OFFICER.

VOLUME V

WAR DIARY or INTELLIGENCE SUMMARY

Army Form C. 2113.

Place	Date	Hour	Summary of Events and Information	Remarks and references to Appendices
	1917.			
LYTHAM CAMP	FEBY 1		On the morning of the 1st February the Battalion was relieved in R.2 Sub-sector and marched to billets in LYTHAM CAMP. The day was spent in cleaning up generally. Companies paraded for rifle inspection.	
Do.	FEBY 2		N:2 supplied a working party of 1 Officer and 20 O.Rs. to 219th Field Coy. R.E. Haversack rations were carried. Bathing was done during the day. On the night of 2nd/3rd the Battalion relieved the 11th Border Regiment in R. SUBSECTOR. Colonel No. 2 Paul was admitted to F.A. Major J.A. Mann took over Command of the Battalion.	
TRENCHES	FEBY 3		N:2 sent out 2 Patrols each consisting of 1 Officer 1 Sergeant and 5 O.Rs. to locate and report on enemy positions. 1st patrol left POLLS PERCH on a bearing of 29° magnetic for 100 yards then proceeded EAST for 400 yards on a bearing of 92° magnetic. Patrol proceeded to Eastern End of GLORY LANE. 2nd patrol left FIG POST on a bearing of 8° magnetic for 300 yards to reconnoitre the enemies positions.	
Do.	FEBY 4		In the early morning our B Coy had a faint attack on part 55 in co-operation with the ROYAL NAVAL DIVISION who were carrying out an attack on our right. B Coy after going 50 yards beyond GUN POST were met with heavy machine gun fire from both left and right flanks also assisted by enemy barrage of shrapnel. Owing to the clear visibility of the night it was deemed advisable not to continue any further and the Command	

Army Form C. 2113.

WAR DIARY
or
INTELLIGENCE SUMMARY.
(Erase heading not required.)

Place	Date	Hour	Summary of Events and Information	Remarks and references to Appendices
TRENCHES	FEBY 5.		withdraws to our original front line trench was given by the officer in charge of the operations, and it was carried out in good order, only 3 casualties being reported both from machine gun fire. In the evening our front line and posts were subjected to a Heavy Artillery Barrage.	
			(B. In the morning from about 2 A.M. till 11 A.M. our front line and posts were heavily shelled. The enemy also sent over a lot of tear shells which burst all around our posts. On account of an expected counter attack, Companies stood too in their various posts, in the evening we were relieved in R1 SUBSECTOR by the 16th Lancashire Fusiliers the relief was completed by midnight. —	
-do-	FEBY 6		After being relieved by the 16th Lancashire Fusiliers we withdrew to our camp in BEAUMONT HAMEL and relieved the 2nd K.O.Y.L.I. The relief was completed by 1 A.M. The Battalion supplied carrying parties & draft of 4 2 O R's carried for duty with the Battalion 4 O R's to 2nd Corps School ENGLAND.	
-do-	FEBY 7		The Battalion supplied carrying parties and also working parties. On the night of 7/8 we relieved the 16th H.L.I. in R 2 SUBSECTOR. — our C Coy taking over the posts.	
-do-	FEBY 8		Companies supplied carrying parties, strengthened posts, dug latrines and cleared part of front line trench. We carried out a relief on night of 8/9. 2nd Col. relieving C Coy on the posts.	

Army Form C. 2118.

WAR DIARY
or
INTELLIGENCE SUMMARY.
(Erase heading not required.)

Place	Date	Hour	Summary of Events and Information	Remarks and references to Appendices
TRENCHES	FEBY 9		Patrols were sent out to reconnoitre and locate the exact dispositions of the enemy. Wire also strengthened and roads during to them being blown in. Our B.Coy relieved D.Coy on the posts on the night of 9/10th	MWG
-Do-	FEBY 10		On the night of 10th/11th our R.Coy relieved B Coy in the Posts, and D. Coy withdrew and stood too in close support. C Coy the 1/5th Border Regiment under orders to move at any moment if such support should be required. D.Coy also stood too in close support to 2nd K.O.Y.L.I. under orders to move at any moment if such support should be required. Casualties were as follows 2nd Lieut. A.P. Moon wounded, 1 OR died of wounds, and 8. OR wounded. N°5 Furnished escorts for prisoners. 2 Lieut N.E. Williams on Reinforcement	MWG
-Do-	FEBY 11		Companies supplied carrying parties and clearing trenches which had been blown in. N°5 furnished escorts for prisoners.	MWG
-Do-	FEBY 12		The Battalion relieved the 2nd K.O.Y.L.I. in TENTREE and LAGGER ALLEYS in the morning. Our Casualties were as follows:- Capt. A.E. Marshall and 2nd Lieut F.M.L. Smith killed, also 1 OR killed and 8 ORs wounded. N°5 sent out a patrol to locate the exact position of a German Post which we intended attacking in the morning - 2nd Lieut W.G. Bing and 2nd Lieut Josh Paterson Reinforcements & ORs to Cadet School ENGLAND.	MWG

Army Form C. 2118.

WAR DIARY
or
INTELLIGENCE SUMMARY.
(Erase heading not required.)

Instructions regarding War Diaries and Intelligence Summaries are contained in F. S. Regs., Part II. and the Staff Manual respectively. Title pages will be prepared in manuscript.

Place	Date	Hour	Summary of Events and Information	Remarks and references to Appendices
TRENCHES	FEBY 13		At 4.30 am C Coy made an attack on an enemy post but before reaching the post they were met by the enemy who were superior in numbers, and C Coy were forced to fall back. The Germans managed to occupy our posts but were reinforced C Coy with part of A Coy and 2 platoons of 2nd KOYLI and not successfully counter attacked and drove the enemy back to his original position. The same night we were relieved in TENTREE and LAGGER ALLEYS by 2nd KOYLI. On being relieved the Battalion marched to billets in MAILLY MAILLET. Casualties 4 ORs killed 15 ORs wounded 2nd Lt Butler wounded & missing 9 missing including 2nd Lt Sons support to 2nd KOYLI	MAILLY MAILLET. Being A Coy in
MAILLY MAILLET	FEBY 14		MAILLY MAILLET and marched to hut at BOLTON CAMP. Captain R L Scally MC 2nd Manchester Regiment assumed temporary command of the Battalion. The day was spent cleaning up etc.	the Battalion on the afternoon of Feb 14 at about 4 pm. 2/Lt Veitch MC
BOLTON CAMP	FEBY 15		Companies continued cleaning up and inspections were held under Company arrangements. 2nd Lieut S L Brodie Reinforcement	Veitch
-Do-	FEBY 16		The Battalion was inspected in full marching order by the Commanding Officer. Bathing was carried out during the day.	Veitch

WAR DIARY or INTELLIGENCE SUMMARY

Army Form C. 2113.

Place	Date	Hour	Summary of Events and Information	Remarks and references to Appendices
BOLTON CAMP	FEB 14		The Battalion moved from Bolton Camp to Billets in Mollens-au-Bois. Three 2 O.R's to Cadet School ENGLAND	
MOLLIENS-AU-BOIS	FEB 18		The Battalion paraded for Church parade at 10.30 am. Companies completed cleaning up. Billet areas cleaned up and rubbish disposed of. 2 O.R's to Cadet School ENGLAND	
-do-	FEB 19		Companies paraded for Physical Drill, Close Order Drill and Kitrand exercises. The Battalion paraded at 11.30 am and Capt A.J. Scully M.C. handed over same to Major F.F. Sworder who assumed temporary command from this date. Captain A.J. Scully M.O. was struck off the strength of the Battalion. A draft of 12 O.R's arrived for duty with the Battalion. Capt. Major Temp. agreed	
-do-	FEB 20		Inspection of Billets and Physical Training. Bombing was carried out under Instructors. Companies paraded for Musketry, Squad Drill, Bayonet fighting and Close order drill. A Football match was arranged with 219th Field Coy R.E. but owing to weather conditions it was postponed. A draft of 9 O.R's arrived for duty with this Battalion	
-do-	FEB 21		The Battalion marched from Mollens-au-Bois to Billets in CAMON	

Army Form C. 2118.

WAR DIARY
or
INTELLIGENCE SUMMARY.
(Erase heading not required.)

Instructions regarding War Diaries and Intelligence Summaries are contained in F. S. Regs., Part II. and the Staff Manual respectively. Title pages will be prepared in manuscript.

Place	Date	Hour	Summary of Events and Information	Remarks and references to Appendices
CAMON	FEBY 22.		The battalion marched from CAMON to billets in WIENCOURT.	WWW
WIENCOURT	FEBY 23.		Companies paraded for inspections and cleaned up generally. NCO detailed a fatigue party of 1 NCO and 6 men to report for work with the TOWN MAYOR. A draft of 131 OR's arrived for duty with the battalion.	WWW
-Do-	FEBY 24.		Companies paraded for Bombing, Bayonet fighting and close order drill. Men of the last two drafts were inspected by the Commanding Officer. 1 OR to Cadet School ENGLAND.	WWW
-Do-	FEBY 25.		The battalion marched from WIENCOURT to billets in LE QUESNEL. 1 OR to WWW	WWW
LE QUESNEL -Do-	FEBY 26.		Paraded under Company arrangements cleaning up etc. —	WWW
-Do-	FEBY 27.		Companies paraded for inspection of billets, Physical training, Bombing, Bayonet fighting and close order drill. Commanding Officers Parade, (1) Promulgation of Court-Martial was ordered today (11) Battalion drill.	WWW
-Do-	FEBY 28.		The battalion paraded in full marching order as strong as possible for inspection by G.O.C. 32nd Division. After inspecting companies did Physical training, Bombing, Bayonet fighting and close order drill. A draft of 5 O.R's & 16 attd 6¢1 for duty with the battalion. 1 OR to Cadet School ENGLAND. —	WWW

W. J. R. Williams Capt & Lieut
Intelligence Officer

Vol 17

CONFIDENTIAL

WAR DIARY

FROM 1ST MARCH TO 31ST MARCH 1919.

F.E. Lindsmeur(?)
2nd Lieut.
Intelligence Officer
17th D.H.L.I.

VOLUME No VI

Army Form C. 2118

WAR DIARY
or
INTELLIGENCE SUMMARY
(Erase heading not required.)

Instructions regarding War Diaries and Intelligence Summaries are contained in F. S. Regs., Part II. and the Staff Manual respectively. Title Pages will be prepared in manuscript.

Place	Date	Hour	Summary of Events and Information	Remarks and references to Appendices
LE QUESNEL	1.3.17		Reveille 7 a.m., Breakfast 8 a.m. During the day the routine as noted in Programme of Work was carried through under Company arrangement.	J.E.D.
LE QUESNEL	2.3.17		Reveille 7 a.m., Breakfast 8 a.m. Blankets were stored preparatory to the battalion moving into the line. At 2-30 p.m. the Battalion left its quarters and proceeded to BEAUFORT where packs were stored. Later it moved into the trenches east of ROUVROY and Battalion Headquarters were established at NEY POST. The conditions on taking over from 16th N.F. was active; a heavy swing shell fire being on the front and communication trenches. Unfortunately 1 R/Sgt. and 6 men were returned as casualties on entry; the first being killed and the others wounded by grenade fire. The stores and transport took up quarters at BEAUFORT.	J.E.D.
NEY POST	3.3.17		Battalion was holding right sub sector of Brigade line, with 16th H.L.I. on the left, XI Border Regt. in support at KUROPATKIN, and 2nd KOYLI. in reserve at WARVILLERS. All four companies held the front-line. Activity on both sides was moderate in the trenches and our artillery seemed to be registering on various targets during the day with several bursts of rapid fire during the evening. The enemy fired a few shells into ROUVROY and the surrounding roads, but was more active with grenades and spring bombs some of which were of the gas type. During the day great + useful work was done in clearing the trenches, parts of which had considerably suffered as a result of repair. Weather dry and cold; wind, Brisk S.E.	J.E.D.
NEY POST	4.3.17		The work of clearing and repairing trenches was continued and in several parts much had been entirely cleared + communications greatly facilitated. The digging of new latrines started. Work of Intelligence was carried through and made valuable trench information obtained and aerial observation was much in evidence. Two patrols left our lines during the night to reconnoitre No Man's Land on the immediate front. Weather: bright sunshine during the day with heavy snowfall lasting fully 1 hour during night.	J.E.D.
NEY POST	5.3.17		Work of clearing and repairing trenches and repairing trenches and making new latrines was continued but with much slower progress owing to the melting snow. Artillery activity was decidedly greater on both sides, while Trench Mortars were used by the enemy against our front line; many of the latter missiles contained gas. Aerial Darts were more against our support line. In the evening Battalion was relieved by XI Borders and took up position of Brigade support on trenches. Relief was completed by 11 p.m. without incident. Batt. Headqrs. A + C Coys. established Quarters at KUROPATKIN, B Coy. in Aug outs at ROUVROY and D Coy. at St NICOLAS POST in the rear of left battalion.	J.E.D.

1875 Wt. W593/826 1,000,000 4/15 J.B.C. & A. A.D.S.S./Forms/C. 2118.

WAR DIARY or INTELLIGENCE SUMMARY

Army Form C. 2118

(Erase heading not required.)

Instructions regarding War Diaries and Intelligence Summaries are contained in F.S. Regs., Part II. and the Staff Manual respectively. Title Pages will be prepared in manuscript.

Place	Date	Hour	Summary of Events and Information	Remarks and references to Appendices
KUROPATKIN	6.3.17		Battalion supplied two companies for trench clearing &c. under R.E. while the others cleaned rifles & equipment at this new post. Little or no enemy shelling was directed though there is evidence that at some previous date the immediate vicinity had received the attention of enemy artillery. This was a fairly quiet day for little sign of artillery; that of the enemy being directed principally to the roads and battery emplacements in ROUVROY sector. 50 "heavies" (a large proportion being lachrymatory shells) fell. Weather bright sunshine. Our aeroplanes carried out observation during the morning and some black shrapnel was directed against them with a wonderful mis-judgment of range.	2 E.P.
KUROPATKIN	7.3.17		During the day enemy aircraft was inactive at an altitude task of cleaning trenches; two companies working to Brigade orders and the others to those issued by battalion. Our gas guard and the mouth proved a fair success. Again in the early morning our aeroplanes were active and drew the machines patrolled the line. Enemy artillery light and heavy undecidedly attention to ROUVROY and a fair proportion of the shells were lachrymatory. Weather: bright at first, during later with slight snow fall and keen frost at night.	2 E.P.
KUROPATKIN	8.3.17		Battalion supplied two companies for trench clearing, while the other two companies were engaged carrying stores, preparing to moving into the line. At 5 p.m. the relief of the XI Borders was started and at 10.15 p.m. it was completed. One was less than usual. During the night a remarkable quietude reigned over the trenches and even the shelling of the rear was less than usual. 2 patrols left our lines and carried out a fairly good examination of enemy wire. Weather: bright, clear and frosty with a gentle breeze blowing towards night.	2 E.P.
NEY POST	9.3.17		During the day battalion continued the work of cleaning trenches and repairing posts. At night all companies were engaged during the sap and front line. A small patrol left D Coy and examined the jumping off trench in their front. Enemy activity was much more in evidence than usual and heavy Trench Mortar, Rifle Grenades, and Gas Shells fell while visitating regularly on our front line. Though of long duration this bombardment was not intense and the damage was less than might have been expected. Our enemy suffered at several points and some casualties occurred: Wounded, 6 OR; gassed (slightly) 2 OR; S.S., W.1 OR. Shelling of the rear was heavy at times and much gas was thrown into ROUVROY.	2 E.P.
NEY POST	10.3.17		Of senior officers and captain at our left to join 15TH H.L.I. Weather: Fresh with gentle N.E. wind. The following after first undeed hardly our trenches and much debris was necessary to keep the trenches clear; all companies were engaged on this task during the day. Wiring was strengthened by all companies. P.T.O.	2 E.D.

1875 Wt. W593/826 1,000,000 4/15 J.B.C. & A. A.D.S.S/Forms/C.2118.

WAR DIARY or INTELLIGENCE SUMMARY

Army Form C. 2118

Place	Date	Hour	Summary of Events and Information	Remarks and references to Appendices
NEY POST	10.3.17 (contd)		Enemy shelling continued as our journey day and ROUVROY ROAD suffered much from gas shells. A considerable number of trench mortars were thrown into our lines but the evacuation went not heavy only 2 men being wounded. Gas shells fell on our lines though not in sufficient numbers to become of more than local danger. One machine gun was damaged and put out of action but another was immediately drawn from store in its place. Weather: dull and moist with a damp mist reducing observation difficult. Wind: S.E gentle.	4 E.D
NEY POST	11.3.17		Amongst a further freshening of the atmosphere conditions worked again on the trenches went in many parts the trenches fell in. Every available man was set to work clearing the obstructions and much improvement was obtained. Enemy artillery was quieter than usual though about 6pm a very heavy bombardment was observed some distance on the right. Aeroplane observation was carried out by our machines in the morning and about 11am a German bi-plane was driven off by the fire of our artillery. Our 4.2" and 6" howo played havoc on the enemy frontline and silenced the German T.M which had so actively bombarded our line during the past two days. Our S.I.W. was reported during the day. A patrol left our lines about midnight and returned having completely completed their work and returned 2 hours later without incident. Weather fine, gentle S.E wind freshening.	4 E.D
NEY POST	12.3.17		forty reporting their work and returned 2 hours later without incident. Weather fine, gentle S.E wind freshening. The day opened with drenching rain and a fresh wind setting towards N as the day progressed. The rain had serious effect on the trenches, many parts falling in and causing obstructions. During the day every effort was made to clear the main trenches in view of the relief arrived to take place in the evening. Our 18 pounders opened fire on FOUQUESCOURT about 4am and continued to send occasional shots to their mark till 6am. In the afternoon our How began to play on the enemy front line and wire; the shooting continued all evening and appeared to attain the desired effect. At 6.15 p.m. one enterprise by our artillery to draw the enemy fire led to a slight retaliation. Whether the full disposition of the enemy gun strength was revealed or not is difficult to say but his reply was few shots of reparations - about 10 No 4.2" shells, 15 No. heavy T.M, and several small arms being directed against our front line. These mostly fell about GB1, a point which has received much attention from the enemy. May be the decidedly moderate intensity of our own fire accounted for the absence of reply. After this the relief was started and the 2/12am the XII borders Ltd. took over from the Batln no trouble incident. The Battalion evacuated its Headquarters at KUROPATKIN and S.W. being towards N. Weather. Mild with intervals of bright sunshine.	4 E.D
KUROPATKIN	13.3.17		Battalion in Brigade Support. During the afternoon two Coys formed working parties under supervision of R.E. and according to Brigade orders. Their duties consisted of clearing & occupied portion of the trenches. An urgent order requiring the return of Lewis Guns	4 E.D

1875 Wt. W⁵93/826 1,000,000 4/15 J.B.C. & A. A.D.S.S./Forms/C. 2118.

WAR DIARY or INTELLIGENCE SUMMARY

Army Form C. 2118

(Erase heading not required.)

Place	Date	Hour	Summary of Events and Information	Remarks and references to Appendices
KUROPATKIN	13.3.19 cont		to Brigade Store carried back to be brought from BEAUFORT and dumped in ROUVROY where they was distributed to their individual owners. Thereafter tasks were changed and the transport carried the Gunn Boots to Brigade Store accompanied by a fatigue party from B Coy who unloaded the limber and washed the boots. Enemy observation aircraft had a good point of vantage in this part because men crossing towards the Dumps were repeatedly shelled. Weather dull with intermittent showers of rain. Latterly breaking into a constant drizzle. Wind SSW gentle.	F & Q
do	14.3.19		Battalion supplied two companies at working parties under the Supervision of R.E. while the others were engaged under Battalion arrangements clearing KUROPATKIN TRENCH (much of which had fallen in with the rain) and clearing the vicinity of Dugouts and old rubbish. In the latter part of the day stores were dumped according to Brigade Orders and at 4.30pm the Relief with 1st Dorsets commenced. At 9.30pm the relief was complete without incident and the Battalion returned to billets in LE QUESNEL.	F & Q
LE QUESNEL	15.3.19		Reveille 7am, Breakfast 8am. The early part of the day was fully occupied in cleaning rifles, equipment and clothing. A Company inspection parade was held by each Coy Commander. In the evening the C.O lectured to officers and N.C.Os on General Routine and Discipline: paying particular attention to the benefits of treating men with encouragement and means less liable to be taken in offence than with bullying and whining.	F & Q
do	16.3.19		Reveille 6am, Breakfast 7.45am. Work according to Company arrangements and programme of work was started at 9am and carried later owing to rifle range being at the Battalions disposal. Two Coy's fired on the Ranges while others carried out squad drill, bombing and elementary musketry. In the afternoon a rich verra arrangement was carried through. In the evening orders were issued arranging for battalion to move in relief to 96th Brigade in pursuit of retiring enemy.	F & Q
do	17.3.19		Battalion moved off and at 2.15am Headquarters were fully established at BOUCHOIR. Stores were left at LE QUESNEL but first line transport accompanied the Battalion during this day. Our "A" Scouts going in and around BOUCHOIR fired mostly.	F & Q

WAR DIARY or INTELLIGENCE SUMMARY

Army Form C. 2118

Place	Date	Hour	Summary of Events and Information	Remarks and references to Appendices
LE QUESNEL	14/3/19 Contd.		increasing regularity on the probable localities of the enemy, only stopping at night when there was no sound of warfare was silent	F & Q
BOUCHOIR	18/3/19		In the early morning Brigade orders arrived instructing the Battalion to move. At 9.30 am this Battalion left BOUCHOIR and proceeded through LE QUESNOY EN SANTERRE to the old British front line. Battalion Headquarters were established at CASTELUAU – WORK and the companies occupied the line. At 5 pm the move was continued through the much extinguished and ruined villages of PARVILLERS, BATELFELD, by the Germans and the Battalion rested for the night at FRESNOY-LES-ROYE. The habits of this front was remarkably good considering the so recent occupation of an enemy force and the most of the road surface in NO MANS LAND left little to be desired. FRESNOY had suffered severely from shell fire, aided by wanton and prepared destructiveness of the enemy. The move finished at 10 pm.	F & Q
FRESNOY	19/3/19		9am of this day saw us once more paraded for further marching and at 9.30am the Battalion moved off in divisional reserve on roads for ETALON. This march was carried through in an atmosphere of peaceful quietude and in a perfect day, making war appear more as a thought than an actual and existing condition. Hence of the silence and atmospheric conditions tended to to little the suffering of war. Here were abundant signs of the methodical destruction of a receding enemy. Everything ruined everywhere in or near CREMERY which we passed through. Les in ETALON where we rested. Fruit trees were cut down, walls were destroyed or entrenched. Houses were razed to the ground and in many cases the surrounding ruined showed how recently had been the evacuation. In south cases the obstructing must have been larger than our front line troops 144th & 96th Brigades because telegraph poles had been cut down. The tops remained of sufficient lengths and clear geometry for re-erection. The railway line though severely damaged was far from finally ruined and the roads though harassed and rutted were not sufficiently defaced to reviewing troops at ETALON this Battalion took up billets about 12:45pm and immediately sent out No1 Platoon on OUTPOST Duty while visual signalling parties Reset up communication between the trenches	F & Q

WAR DIARY or INTELLIGENCE SUMMARY

Army Form C. 2118

Place	Date	Hour	Summary of Events and Information	Remarks and references to Appendices
FRESNOY	19.3.17 Contd		and the man body. At 4.30 a.m. another order was received and by 5 a.m. the Battalion had left ETALON for the more comfortable quarters of NESLE. Along this route the burning of houses was more prevalent and though civilians had mostly been in small villages & gave in the farmhouses, the whole system was such destruction. Town destroyed at the entrance seemed to have quite this enemy's more serious thought than Nikita and burnt craters spoke to the garrison nature of their intention. Tickets, the nearer we were for from successful and excepting the bridging of the various rivers of Somme in the main street no serious obstruction appeared to have occurred. The Battalion rested at NESLE where quite a number of civilians remained. The Battalion being able to live at an immediate resort and under no orders to move spent the	(?)
NESLE	20.3.17		day resting and cleaning. During and much time as possible to the improving of Billets, construction of latrines and organising transport for further advance. The day passed without incident. A factory building served as a barracks and easily accommodated the four companies.	(?)
-do-	21.3.17		Reveille 6.30 a.m. Breakfast 7 a.m. Battalion still resting in NESLE L. The forenoon two companies were employed repairing damaged roads and there was a relieving by the other two companies in the afternoon. Later urgent orders were received taking a party to be sent to a bridge on the outskirts of the town where work of clearing away debris was carried on. This bridge must have been blown by the enemy and owing to debris forming a dam the water of the river at 11 a.m. threatens to inundate much of the neighbourhood.	(?)
-do-	22.3.17		Battalion at NESLE NEUVILLE 6.30 a.m. Breakfast 7.30 a.m. The event of repairing roads round NESLE was carried on and roads in Battalion allotted areas were cleaned. Companies west on fatigue another Coy. arrangements and Bayonet fighting and Close order drill were practiced. On this day the hand made a start with retreat much to the satisfaction of the natives who showed great interest and pleasure at the band marches from Headquarters Billets to St Louis	(?)

WAR DIARY
or
INTELLIGENCE SUMMARY
(Erase heading not required.)

Army Form C. 2118

Place	Date	Hour	Summary of Events and Information	Remarks and references to Appendices
NESLE	22.3.19		Last Headquarters fell and back again. A heavy shower of snow fell at dusk but later the atmosphere though sharp chill remained fair.	034
-Do-	23.3.19		Battalion at NESLE. Brigade working parties were found by all companies, C Coy and two platoons of D Coy being employed digging a channel for sewer near ROUY-LE-PETIT ROAD, two platoons of B were left there for work of repairing bridge at GRAND PLACE NESLE & the afternoon A Coy and part of B relieved C & D Coys. Wheat again forward interest to the population.	J34
-Do-	24.3.19		The Battalion in NESLE. B Coy supplied three fatigue parties under supervision of R.E. as follows:– 1) NESLE BRIDGE at ROUY LE PETIT. C + D Coys were engaged in working parties and Battalion duties and details found parties to work six hour shift from 9pm of this date till 9am next day. This party was under orders of 256 Tunnelling Coy R.E. at a event near Railway Bridge on ROUY LEPETIT road. A Coy relieved 16 th H.L.I. Piquets at ..... Sauvis Barn and four plenty task for 24 hours. Amount of more than usual importance took place in NESLE. President POINCARE visited the town and was received by an Guard of Honour .... while the music was supplied by the combined bands of 16 th and 14 th H.L.I. Pipes band. The enthusiasm of the reception was extremely moderate and seemed to signify the after math of two years forced existence of the enemy. The populace whereas in the square and ...... 500 persons gazed of a fair number of British Soldiers. The youth of the .... was conspicuous in its absence.	034

WAR DIARY or INTELLIGENCE SUMMARY

Army Form C. 2118.

Instructions regarding War Diaries and Intelligence Summaries are contained in F.S. Regs., Part II. and the Staff Manual respectively. Title pages will be prepared in manuscript.

(Erase heading not required.)

Place	Date	Hour	Summary of Events and Information	Remarks and references to Appendices
NESLE	25.3.17		The Battalion at NESLE N to relieved 6 Coy of Regiment duty around NESLE and MESNIL ST NICAISE. Battn to supplied the following working parties. 6am 2 offrs 100 O.R.	4 & D
			100 O. Ranks at HESSIAN BRIDGE north-west of ROUY LE GRAND 6am. 2 officers 100 other ranks at CANAL BRIDGE north-east of ROUY LE GRAND on East bank of the SOMME. 12 noon. Two parties composed of about relieved. These 8am 2 N.C.O.s and 30 men at NESLE BRIDGE near ST LEONARD. These were carried out under the instructions of R.E.	
-do-	26.3.17		The Battalion at NESLE C. completed 75 O.R. in present duty. Battalion supplied the following working parties 4 officers 150 other ranks at CANAL handly each of ROUY-LE-GRAND 12 hours duty of same strength relieved the above 8am. 2 officers and 100 other ranks at CANAL BRIDGE OFFOY. This working party carried out work under direction of R.E. Battalion at NESLE 8am. 2 officers and 50 other ranks. Battalion supplied the following working parties 8am. 4 officers 200 O.R. at Canal each R of ROUY-LE-GRAND 12 hours of party composed and strength we three like and shortly twelve and carried out work under direction of R.E.	4 & D
-do-	27.3.17		The Battalion at NESLE. King the day Battalion Headquarters 11-15am. 12 noon. Battalion moved to a starting point proceeding to proceeding to being to position on east side of HESSIAN ROAD. We moved by the NE bank of NESLE along the road to Bridge & Canal, through on to Road & main to VOYENNES this village the march of telephones led the Battn ordered out to cross a greater ball of the road making of the bridge over the Battn halted. Many huts were to be meaned in the village then VOYENNES the Battalion marched down the north bank of the CANAL OFFOY BRIDGE & thence to OFFOY everything was on the march till arrived BRIDGE the ??? of the ran across the bridge east of through this destruction of R? from Bridge no difficulty was experienced to held on east side VOYENNES to reach a level of 30 yards was formed through a voyage made the NE to Halt. Gilbert to TOULLE where the ??? were to be held unit for the party Battn marched off this to at 6 hours the accompanied through DOILLY and FORESTS to GERMAINE mostly of the men were ??? within half an hour ??? ??? ??? for the night Battn bivouaced NE of TOULLE wait made at all GERMAINE KN (?) ... ... when all made. An enemy aerodrome was noted ??? ... ... (?) aeroplanes and carried out from 9am till 4pm. 3 Coys learned half R and one batts ??? ??? ??? ??? held in the St GERMAINE V. of IV Casltr Cavalry Brigade staff, morning	4 & D

Army Form C. 2118.

WAR DIARY
or
INTELLIGENCE SUMMARY.

(Erase heading not required.)

Instructions regarding War Diaries and Intelligence Summaries are contained in F. S. Regs., Part II. and the Staff Manual respectively. Title pages will be prepared in manuscript.

Place	Date	Hour	Summary of Events and Information	Remarks and references to Appendices
GERMAINE	29.3.19		Battalion at GERMAINE. Bugling was continued by the Companies. — Night operations was cancelled about 9 p.m. and the Battalion instructed to await further orders.	⅔ ①
So. -	30.3.19		Battalion at GERMAINE. Various route march disarmament and the Companies practised extended order drill. the Central Roads were guarded by a patrol from Battalion at GERMAINE.	⅔ ②
So. -	31.3.19		Had marches by preview the Battalion. Central posts. Battalion stood to waiting orders to move. Companies finished making company arrangements for inspections.	⅔ ③

CONFIDENTIAL

Vol 18

17TH H.L.I.

WAR DIARY

FROM

1ST TO 30TH APRIL

1917

VOL. No. 6.

W.M. Ashurst. Captain.
Adjutant 17th Battalion
Highland Light Infantry.

WAR DIARY
or
INTELLIGENCE SUMMARY.

(Erase heading not required.)

Army Form C. 2118.

Place	Date	Hour	Summary of Events and Information	Remarks and references to Appendices
GERMAINE & SAVY	1.4.17		Battalion moved off from GERMAINE at midnight and proceeded by companies across country to FLUQUIERES. During this we passed through the village – a file of men – and from thence to their ST QUENTIN road. About 400 yds along this road we arrived ROUPY and at the cross roads totally destroyed by barrage turned along the VAUX road and later proceeded along SAVY road. NE of the ROUPY cemetery and on the SW side of the road running into SAVY battalion took up position of deployment with A and B coys in two waves 20 yards apart (A being on the right and B on the left) and covering a front of 400 yards. C Company followed in the third wave and D Company in the fourth, both companies being extended over the battalion frontage. At 5 a.m. with the first burst of barrage fire from our guns, the attack moved forward and shortly afterwards without much opposition gained access to SAVY. In the village some serious opposition was met and since fighting took place in the neighbourhood of the railway bank N of the village. Most of the fighting took place in the neighbourhood of the railway bank N of the village and beyond the railway bank N of the village. Most of the fighting took place in the neighbourhood of the village at the northern end of the village and here the VI BORDERS joined our forces on the left and helped to push the enemy back. Once through the village serious destruction was caused by heavy machine gun fire. An enemy strong point established in a crater on the right bank night at once reorganised and with the aid of two Lewis guns skilfully manipulated, the crater was soon in our hands and a heavy fire directed against the retreating enemy. C Company had now changed direction and formed a protection to our right flank by forming a line facing East. Thereafter the battalion started to dig in – about 6-30 a.m. – and own a comparatively wide area of front our support trenches running throughout the day enemy artillery showed great activity against the village and ROUPY – SAVY road, while snipers, machine guns, and some artillery played on the battalion frontier. The work of attending the wounded was carried out in an advanced post in SAVY while the advance to FA was attended to until communication forming trains considering the large number of cases and the distance to be traversed. The brigade at this time was disposed as follows:– 17th H.L.I. and XI Borders holding village and support SAVY and 16th H.L.I. in reserve at VAUX.	

WAR DIARY
or
INTELLIGENCE SUMMARY.

(Erase heading not required.)

Army Form C. 2118.

Instructions regarding War Diaries and Intelligence Summaries are contained in F. S. Regs., Part II. and the Staff Manual respectively. Title pages will be prepared in manuscript.

Place	Date	Hour	Summary of Events and Information	Remarks and references to Appendices
SAVY	1.4.17		In the afternoon a further advance was made by the 96th Brigade, and before evening BOIS DE SAVY was in our hands. The Brigade having passed through as the battalion was resting in the evening and dug B form all companies advanced in off to take up quarters in dug-outs on the FLUQUIERES-DOUCHY road. The accommodation in these quarters proved to be totally inadequate owing to the drawing near of the relieving enemy and a large portion of the battalion bivouacked. The casualties for the day totally 103, 31 of whom were killed. Capt Brigdale was wounded on this day and died from wounds some days later.	
FLUQUIERES-DOUCHY RD	2.4.17		Battalion in quarters and bivouacks, and held in readiness to proceed to take near action in the storming of BOIS D'HOLNON. Later in the day information was received that this operation had been completed by the 11th Brigade followed by 2nd KOYLI who gained touch on the left with the 1st Division. at this stage orders were received asking two working parties for digging in were send. These were duly supplied + carried through. They were only casually, resulting from hands dropped by enemy aircraft. The remainder of the battalion were engaged cleaning equipment + clothing.	
FLUQUIERES-DOUCHY RD.	3.4.17		Battalion in dug-outs and bivouacks. During the night the weather became extremely cold and the men suffered from exposure in the scanty shelter at their disposal. The weather improved during the day and every effort was made to improve the dug-outs. In the afternoon the French attacked on our right + captured DALLON at a slight cost. C Coy moved their quarters to renovated cellars in FLUQUIERES.	
FLUQUIERES-DOUCHY RD	4.4.17		Heavy rain fell during the evening and nearly all dug-outs and shelters leaked badly. Battalion in dug-outs and bivouacs. Owing to snow and rain the companies suffered and B Coy. changed quarters and occupied cellars in FLUQUIERES. The number of the battalion were engaged in Coy. parades and further improvements to dug-outs and bivouacs. Battalion ordered to move to attack FAYET on the following day. In the afternoon the orders for attack were cancelled and battalion remained in readiness.	

Army Form C. 2118.

WAR DIARY
or
INTELLIGENCE SUMMARY.

(Erase heading not required.)

Instructions regarding War Diaries and Intelligence Summaries are contained in F.S. Regs., Part II. and the Staff Manual respectively. Title pages will be prepared in manuscript.

Place	Date	Hour	Summary of Events and Information	Remarks and references to Appendices
FLUQUIERES – DOUCHY RD	5.6.17		Battalion in Aug. huts and bivouacs. Dead horses lying in surrounding fields were buried. Shrapnel & such was received from General SHUTE and Brigadier BLACKLOCK and later in the day orders were issued that battalion would move to GERMAINE. The move took place accordingly and by 9pm battalion was established in GERMAINE.	
GERMAINE & FRANCILLY SELENCY	6.6.17		Battalion in billets. The early part of the day was taken up with cleaning and a battalion parade was called for 2pm. This parade was cancelled and inspection under company arrangements was substituted. Hungerton battalion prepared to move into Brigade support and greatcoats were handed in to R.M. Stores. At 6pm a move towards the line commenced under the command of Capt. PATERSON M.C. thereout. Forward was through VAUX, ETRELLERS, + SAVY to FRANCILLY where we relieved the 2nd MANCHESTERS. The march & relief were carried out in a deluge of rain, and conditions for the night were without extremely trying. The defence line held by the battalion ran from FRANCILLY to SELENCY with reserve trenches/supports being the village. Both villages and approaches thereto were heavily shelled by the enemy but the relief was carried through without casualty.	
FRANCILLY SELENCY	7.6.17		Battalion occupying FRANCILLY SELENCY defence line with two companies established in a trench at N.E. corner of FRANCILLY SELENCY. During the day enemy shelling was not intense, continued unabated against the village. It is now well ascertained that shelling was the dumping of a shell at the entrance of our A Coy. cellar. Enemy observation is very clear from the ridge opposite and as a result its artillery fire has a marked accuracy with machine gun fire from the enemy commands a large portion of the surrounding ground. Sniping is carried on from the lines but will now no actions would serve purpose. A Coy. lies in front of the village of the line, D, B + C Coys. following in the order named push left. 16 the N.F. into the line on night of battalion and 2nd KOYLI was stationed on our left. At 10pm a Coy of KOYLI attacked and captured 3 cottages from the enemy without meeting any serious defence. The attack proved quickset without any additional shelling through M.G. fire was heard in immediate vicinity. A patrol Lieut. Sewtice to reconnoitre enemy lines last after proceeding a considerable distance towards FAYET was forced to return under fire from German field guns. Major LUMSDEN D.S.O. (with bar) joined battn and assumed command in absence of Col SWORDER who returned + GERMAINE. Capt PATERSON M.C.	

WAR DIARY
INTELLIGENCE SUMMARY

Army Form C. 2118.

(Erase heading not required.)

Instructions regarding War Diaries and Intelligence Summaries are contained in F. S. Regs., Part II. and the Staff Manual respectively. Title pages will be prepared in manuscript.

Place	Date	Hour	Summary of Events and Information	Remarks and references to Appendices
FRANCILLY SELENCY	8.4.17		Battalion holding FRANCILLY SELENCY line of defence. Orders were received relating to a proposed attack on FAYET following a French attack on the night and the 61st Div. on the left. This did not materialise and our orders were cancelled. Later instructions called for a reorganisation of the line and this was carried out without hitch by 11-45 p.m. Battalion took over RDV/1 line and with the assistance of 1 Bn XI BORDERS on a support held the Brigade front. A Coy. held the night, with C, B & D coys. forming the line on left in near support held the Brigade front. During the day, Capt. MORTON, 2/Lt. HERRON & 2/Lt. BRESLIN rejoined Battalion. Capt. MORTON took over "B" Coy. and the others were posted to C & B Coys. respectively. During the day 3 casualties were reported: 2/Lt. J. H. SMITH and 2 O.R. being hit by shrapnel at crater in FAYET road. From 8 p.m. till	
FRANCILLY SELENCY	9.4.17		10 join a fire was seen to the burning fiercely in the direction of ROCOURT. Battalion holding Brigade front. Enemy artillery continued to show great activity, shelling our billeted against our lines, FRANCILLY and SELENCY, with increasing regularity during the entire day. Only two sallies seemed to hit on the dot against no. 77 "H" checked from a point not far from and east of FAYET fell in the fields and on our lines while a large number 10.5 ? ? ? ? stello fell in FRANCILLY and some from ST QUENTIN. Another enemy battery firing from direction of GRICOURT fires on the roads and batteries in our rear. During the afternoon some daring reconnaissance was carried out by the patrols following orders issued by Brigade. Four patrols left our lines to gain information of FAYET and the ground between FRANCILLY and ST QUENTIN. A fitting example was set by 2/Lt. DUNSMUIR who accompanied the ground forward to within 400 yds. of the enemy wire round ST. QUENTIN. (Returning to our lines these officers found the body of the late Capt. LINZELL A.D.M.S. This was brought in late by our stretcher bearers and returned to A.D.M.S. Headquarters.) The four patrols carried out other manoeuvres with fair success, one going into the ridge overlooking ST QUENTIN, one going into a German trench near FAYET, one getting within 300 yards of FAYET and the other reconnoitring the southern approaches of the village. The information, although not definite regarding the strength of FAYET garrison, points to there being comparatively few of the enemy along between no mans and ST QUENTIN. 2/Lt. BRESLIN, whose party reconnoitred with commendable gallantry, was menaced by a rifle bullet, but all returned to our lines. During the day some S.A.A.O. work was carried out by our artillery among battalion lists and scouts firing a curious fact at near FAYET	

Also. Ref. A5834 Wt. W4978/M687 750.000 8/16 D. D. & L. Ltd. Forms/C.2118/13.

WAR DIARY
or
INTELLIGENCE SUMMARY.
(Erase heading not required.)

Army Form C. 2118.

Place	Date	Hour	Summary of Events and Information	Remarks and references to Appendices
FRANCILLY SELENCY & HOLNON	10.4.17		Battalion holding Brigade line of defence. During the day enemy artillery showed slightly more activity and most of the shelling fell on unoccupied ground. Two patrols left our lines towards the ground in front. Much good work was accomplished and most useful information regarding enemy strong points, trenches, wiring and movement. Additional to facts of military importance is that of a woman being seen walking in FAYET accompanied by a man dressed in civilian clothing. At night the Battalion was relieved by the XI BORDERS, A.C. & D Coys. and Battn. Hdqrs. re-establishing their quarters in HOLNON while B Coy. remained in close support to XI BORDERS in SELENCY. The relief was carried out without incident by 10-20 p.m., and shortly afterwards the village was subjected to enemy artillery fire. The shelling seemed to be directed chiefly against one of our R.F.A. Batteries situated at N end of village.	
HOLNON	11.4.17		Battalion in HOLNON, B Coy. in Support to BORDERS. During the day cleaning of clothing and equipment was carried out under company arrangement. Beyond some light shells in the morning and a few "strafes" during the day, enemy artillery was quiet. In the evening the shelling commenced although the 18 pdrs. from the village barking constantly, which the "Bosche" retorted onto from the rear and Bois D'HOLNON. During the afternoon a thin cloud of black smoke rose from ST. QUENTIN and continued for fully 15 minutes. A night carrying party from A Coy. was sent to the BORDERS in our front line and 4 men were detailed by C Coy. to assist in mining fatigue. Much work was done during the day to improve existing cellar accommodation, also a mess kitchen & orderly room was erected in close proximity to the officers quarters.	
HOLNON	12.4.17		Battalion in HOLNON, B Coy. in support to BORDERS. Battalion stood to working parties being supplied to assist XI BORDERS in reconnoissance with movement on our flanks. Wiring, carrying parties were supplied to take up duty in Bttn. Hrs. of 14th Inf. Bde. Capt MORTON assumed command of battn. fortwith, Capt PATERSON M.C. being second in command.	

WAR DIARY
or
INTELLIGENCE SUMMARY.

(Erase heading not required.)

Army Form C. 2118.

Place	Date	Hour	Summary of Events and Information	Remarks and references to Appendices
HOLNON	13.4.17		Battalion in HOLNON. 13 Coy being in close support to XI BORDERS. At 7 a.m. a slow barrage fire was put onto ST QUENTIN signifying the advance of the French troops against the town. Our batteries cooperated & smoke-assisted retaliation was meted out to the village. The French frontal attack must culminate. During the day orders were received regarding the offensive to be made against FAYET next morning. C & D Coys. were Lewis gun section to support in the advance to support 2nd K.O.Y.L.I. Lewis Guns were sent at the disposal of officers commanding attack. A Coy. supplied carrying parties to No.6 Coy. attacking [illegible]. B Coy. was held in readiness. At 9 p.m. the above arrangements were terminated and before midnight everything was held in hand. Early in the evening the French made a covert attack on ST QUENTIN but again stay formed their positions too strongly held.	
HOLNON FAYET	14.4.17		Battn. H.Qrs., A & B Coys. in HOLNON; C & D Coys. disposed as above. The artillery kept up an intermittent fire till 4.30 a.m. when the barrage fire opened and stillness aspect of a peaceful spring morning was suddenly disturbed by the increasing hash of guns and swish of shells forming a magnificent barrage on FAYET. This continued for well over an hour, the sounds changing to suit conditions & fortunately an appearance such a prearranged scheme. By means of visual signalling a message was received that the first objective had been gained (the village of FAYET) and an hour afterwards a Brigade message arrived intimating the successful accomplishment at all points. At the arch phone 10th H.L.I. who formed the front line with the 2nd K.O.Y.L.I. on D Coy. were moved up but on reporting they were sent to relieve an C+D with the K.O.Y.L. In the afternoon a further advance was made by the XI BORDERS who met with little or no opposition and by the evening the line of defence occupied lay our front was the ridge from Sug CRICOURT to the junction of FAYET road with the road CRICOURT-ST QUENTIN road. Late in the afternoon orders were received requiring 2 in 3 Coys. to assume duty under command of Capt. MORTON and for two hours reconnaissance was made by Capt. PATERSON M.C. and 2/Lt DUNSMUIR through which advanced parties preparatory organisation and disposition of the Battalion were determined. Volunteers set to and reconnoitred the wires of consolidation enclosing 2/Lt. McIntosh. Casualties reported 2nd Lt R. Cartwright & Cunningham + 23 wounded including 2/Lt. McIntosh.	

A 5834. Wt. W4973/M687. 750,000. 8/16. D.D. & L. Ltd. Forms/C.2118/13.

Army Form C. 2118.

WAR DIARY
or
INTELLIGENCE SUMMARY.
(Erase heading not required.)

Instructions regarding War Diaries and Intelligence Summaries are contained in F. S. Regs., Part II. and the Staff Manual respectively. Title pages will be prepared in manuscript.

Place	Date	Hour	Summary of Events and Information	Remarks and references to Appendices
HOLNON FAYET	15.4.17		Battn. Holnon with A Coy & details. B, C & D Coys holding the line NEW FAYET with 2nd KOYLI. 16th H.L.I. and XI BORDERS. During the day 15th L.F. moved into support in FAYET and 16th L.F. took up their new position in HOLNON. Work of digging the new line was continued and considerable progress was made to the consolidation of the position. During the day messages of congratulation were received from Bde Gen. (BLACKLOCK) General SHUTE, & Gen. RAWLINSON. At 8 p.m. the task of relieving our battalion was continued by the 16th L.F. and by 3 a.m. the last of our coys had arrived at GERMAINE when headquarters were established.	
GERMAINE	16.4.17		Battalion at GERMAINE. During the day 1 platoon was disposed of the Labour Coy at ATTILY. During the day cleaning & equipment was being carried out and inspections under coy arrangements were carried out. Intimation was made during the day that the following divisional honours had been granted to the Battn. for the action at SAVY — 16149 Cpl. H. Shenbourn, 27367 2/Cpl. J Pearson, 23053 Pte G.S. Anderson, 9808 Sgt. J Johnstone, 2727 L/Cpl W Glennie, 2725 L/Sgt. J Ramage, 43219 Pte. R. Yurndult gained Military Medals and 2997 Sgt. R. Lerman gained a bar to his Military Medal won in November. A batt. Church Parade was held at 7 p.m.	
GERMAINE	17.4.17		Battalion at GERMAINE. During the day bath. carried out bathing and cleaning of clothes and equipment. In the afternoon the C.O. held hadre parade at about 5.30 p.m.	
GERMAINE	18.4.17		Battalion at GERMAINE. During the day baths paraded according to orders. Usual coy arrangements were made under coy arrangements. Battn. Orderly Room was held at 5.30 p.m. 13 other thro/hm/m battalion entertainments held in large billet. Orders were issued for one on marches.	
GERMAINE CANIZY	19.4.17		Battalion at GERMAINE. By 9 am coats were packed on transport and fulls marching kit was in readiness. Battn. paraded at 11 a.m. Bus convoy N.E. of GERMAINE the advance of the returning battns. (Gen. Ox and Bucks) Battn. marched off about noon. The route chosen was through DOUILLY and TOULLE. Between which villages dinner was served on route. Continuing via OFFOY, our destination (CANIZY) was reached about 4-10 p.m. This village is void of active population with the exception of one family who returned to their ruined home on the 18th. Destruction by the Germans has been carried out in the same deliberate and wanton scale as in other by the devastations the organised area and what appears to have been the...	

A5834 Wt. W4973 M687 739000 8/16 D. D. & L. Ltd. Forms/C.2118/13.

WAR DIARY
or
INTELLIGENCE SUMMARY.
(Erase heading not required.)

Army Form C. 2118.

Place	Date	Hour	Summary of Events and Information	Remarks and references to Appendices
CANIZY	19.4.17 contd.		pleasant village in fact time was spent and afforded at the main street at the S. end of the village.	[initials]
CANIZY	20.4.17		Battalion at CANIZY. During the day Battalion paraded under routine as set forth in special training scheme. Coys carried out training in close order, physical, bayonet, bombing & bombing over. Battn drill was held at 12 noon and parade finished at 1 pm. During the afternoon the vicinity was reconnoitred with a view to procuring suitable firing grounds for rifle range. Practicable places were examined with the purpose of organising a band.	[initials]
CANIZY	21.4.17		Battalion at CANIZY. Parades were carried out in accordance with the scheme laid down in Brigade Order. Specialists classes have been formed & work is being carried on. In the afternoon a trial football match took place. Coys were employed to assist in clearing a town to play against a French team at HAM. During the new bugle band copied its assistance in playing later. Additional difficulty supplied up during the day; several regular warrants been retained to the village with the intention of procuring what amounts of their homesteads.	[initials]
CANIZY	22.4.17		At 2 p.m. Battalion assembled at railway line South of village and marched off to HAM where a football match was to be displayed by the bugle team. The march was at 115 & on opening articulate and the route march was much enjoyed in the light equipment of belt, bayonet, and rifle with the necessary ammunition carried in the time. We proceeded through EPPEVILLE into HAM where we arrived carried great interest. From our entry into the town till our arrival at the Town Hall our march was through a long line of French soldiers who lined the roads. Several civilians were among the throng. Towards the square the crowd grew denser and in our approach along the main street the square seemed totally blocked with a mass of French soldiers & passages was thought to our view. The magnitude of our reception was thought to our view. A coy of Infantry stood at	[initials]

WAR DIARY or INTELLIGENCE SUMMARY

Army Form C. 2118.

Place	Date	Hour	Summary of Events and Information	Remarks and references to Appendices
CANIZY	22.4.17 (contd)		"Paraed" as guard of Honour whilst we marched passed the Guard Hall. Bath. halted in the square and a French band rendered our National Anthem. After the usual complements had been paid Batln. marched off to the east end of the town where two beautiful football pitches and ground prepared on the canal banks. Our match was against the 121 of Inf. Reg. team but on the field we found another team ready to play our second team (which had no outfit and had to be thrown on the spot). The match against the 121 Reg. our strong team was a very easy victory and now not very winners by 6 goals to 1. The 408 th Reg. team (champions) counted our scrub team great anxiety and a first hand game ended in a draw of 2 goals each. During the game music was discoursed by the French band and our pipers. The French band played the battn. from the football ground to the outskirts of the town and we returned to CANIZY much pleased with the division conferred on us. During the day many inter-coy games graced the proceedings including the General Staffs of French and British troops. A matchee festive was the magnificent reception given to the battn. pipers have whilst playing was received with great favour.	
CANIZY	23.4.17		Batln. at CANIZY. Batln. Orderly Room 6.30 am. During the day programme of work was complied with and battalion paraded accordingly. Batln. Signaller was told by a Div. Sig Officer at BUNY. In the afternoon battalion paraded and received a lecture and demonstration on Gas Attacks, Protective Measures against gas and the use of the Shemlon Horn by the Div. Gas Officer. At 7 pm companies held a musketry parade & rifle inspection. The following officers drew their awarded honours in the recent operations. Capt. J.D. RUSSELL, 2/LT. BRODIE, 2/LT. MARTIN Military Crosses. Capt BLUETT Bar to Military & Cross	

WAR DIARY
or
INTELLIGENCE SUMMARY.
(Erase heading not required.)

Army Form C. 2118.

Place	Date	Hour	Summary of Events and Information	Remarks and references to Appendices
CANIZY	24.4.17	8.30 a.m.	Battalion at CANIZY. Battn Orderly Room 8.30 a.m. Coys carried out parades in accordance with Brigade Training Scheme. In the afternoon the 1st round of the Coys Football Competition was commenced and C Coy beat A Coy by 19 goals to 0.	
CANIZY	25.4.17	8.30 a.m.	Battalion at CANIZY. Battn Orderly Room 8.30 a.m. Coys carried out parades in accordance with Brigade Training Scheme. In the afternoon D Coy fired Grouping Practice on the range which has been made by Lt.Col. SWORDER returned from leave and assumed command of the Battn. Capt MORTON took second in command. Battn Hqrs team beat B Coy in the first rd of Football Competition by 5 goals to 0. Both gained the following awards in the attack on FAYET. Pte SMITH, Pte HOGG, Pte BODDINGTON & L/Cpl ROBINSON, Military Medals.	
CANIZY	26.4.17	8.30 a.m.	Battalion at CANIZY. Battn Orderly Room 8.30 a.m. During the forenoon lecture on Lessons & training Scheme of Advance, Rear and Flank Guards, formation and method of attack were practised. In the afternoon a demonstration of wiring was given by air officers of the R.E. A Coy fired grouping Practice on the range during the afternoon. Transport team beat D Coy in the Semi Football Competition by 6 goals to 0. A successful and enjoyable concert was held in the evening and the proceedings were graced by the presence of Col. SWORDER's officers.	
CANIZY	27.4.17		Battn. at CANIZY. During the forenoon the usual parades were carried through in accordance with training scheme. In the afternoon C Coy fired Grouping Practice on the range. The Semi-final of Football Competition took place in the evening and Battn Hqrs beat C Coy by 3 goals to 0.	
CANIZY	28.4.17		Battalion at CANIZY. During the forenoon parades were carried out in accordance with training Scheme. B Coy fired Grouping Practice on the range. Lieut & Adam from A & C Coys at cricket. A successful Battn concert was held in the evening	

Army Form C. 2118.

WAR DIARY
or
INTELLIGENCE SUMMARY.

(Erase heading not required.)

Instructions regarding War Diaries and Intelligence Summaries are contained in F. S. Regs., Part II. and the Staff Manual respectively. Title pages will be prepared in manuscript.

Place	Date	Hour	Summary of Events and Information	Remarks and references to Appendices
CANIZY.	29.4.17		Battalion at CANIZY. Church Parade conducted 8.30am. In the evening Battn. HdQrs. officiated the Transport in the final of the Football Competition by 3 goals to 0.	
CANIZY	30.4.17	6.15am	Reveille 6am. Parade to march to VOYENNES 6.15am. Battn. marched to VOYENNES where the 99th. Brigade was inspected by General SHUTE the General, in a neat speech after the inspection, complimented the Brigade for the great work it had accomplished in recent operations. In the afternoon Battn. HdQrs. and the Coy. successful shots of the coy. firial grouping Practice on the range. In the evening a start was made with firing a wire for line competition	

CONFIDENTIAL.

17th (S) BATT. HIGHLAND L.I.

WAR DIARY

1st MAY TO 31st MAY 1917.

No. 7.

SIGNATURE _F.E. Dunsmuir, 2/Lieut_
INTELLIGENCE OFFICER

WAR DIARY or INTELLIGENCE SUMMARY

Army Form C. 2118

(Erase heading not required.)

Place	Date	Hour	Summary of Events and Information	Remarks and references to Appendices
CANIZY	1.5.17		Parades were carried out in keeping with the programme of training. In the afternoon A Coy fired Application Practice on the range. In the evening the five-a-side football tournament was continued.	4(E)
CANIZY	2.5.17		Battalion mustered at Crucifix at 8.45am and marched to inspection ground at VOYENNES where 97th Brigade was formed up on three sides of a hollow square at 11am. Inspection was carried out by Army Corps Commander, Sir James Woolcombe, and Div. General Shute assisted by their staff officers. In the afternoon B Coy. fired Application Practice on the range. In the evening Lieu Shute was entertained in Messrs Mess and late attended a ring.	4(E)
CANIZY	3.5.17		Successful Battalion concert. Commanding Officer held a unit parade at 9 am all available ranks being present. Thereafter parades in keeping with the programme of training were carried out, embracing Bombing, Bayonet fighting, Musketry, Physical and Close Order Drill. In the evening the five-a-side tournament was continued.	4(E)
CANIZY	4.5.17		Parades were carried out in keeping with the programme of training, including C Coy's musketry practice on the range. In the afternoon D Coy fired Application Practice on the range. In the evening the Battalion Team beat a team from the 97th M.G.C. at football by 3 goals to 0. Brig Gen Blacklock was entertained in Messrs Mess and later attended a battalion concert.	4(E)
CANIZY	5.5.17		Parades were carried out in keeping with the programme of training. In the afternoon Battn Headquarters fired Application Practice on the range and in the evening further progress was made with the battalion five-a-side football Tournament. Programme and arrangements were drawn up for the battalion Sports to be held on the 6th.	4(E)
CANIZY	6.5.17		Church Parade was held at 9.30am. Owing to unsettled conditions the sports arrangements were altered and only part of the items was carried out. Those were Putting the Weight, 100 yds Heats, Throwing Cricket Ball, Mule Yard Race and Long Jump. The semifinal and final of the Battalion five-a-side football tournament was decided in a win for Transport against Messengers by 1 goal to 0.	4(E)

WAR DIARY
or
INTELLIGENCE SUMMARY

Army Form C. 2118

Instructions regarding War Diaries and Intelligence Summaries are contained in F.S. Regs., Part II. and the Staff Manual respectively. Title Pages will be prepared in manuscript.

(Erase heading not required.)

Place	Date	Hour	Summary of Events and Information	Remarks and references to Appendices
CANIZY	7.5.17		Parades were carried out in keeping with the programme of training. In the afternoon a Start was made with the remainder of the sports programme and by 7 p.m. the meeting was complete. The items entered against events confined to the battalion and others open to the Brigade units. In the later 2nd KOYLI were most successful and one battalion succeeded in winning the final — a relay football tournament. Medals were presented to the winners at the close of the meeting.	4 E.D.
CANIZY	8.5.17		Parades were carried out in keeping with programme of training. In the afternoon A & C Coys fired Rapid Practice on the range. Work of making new turning trenches were continued and further improvements were made to the Range.	4 E.D.
CANIZY	9.5.17		Parades were carried out in keeping with programme of training. Divisional Sports were held in VOYENNES on this date but owing to lack of training no recruits took part from this battalion.	4 E.D.
CANIZY	10.5.17		A & C Coys formed working parties on roads in DOUILLY area. Remainder carried out parades under company arrangements and attended a most interesting lecture & demonstration on Bayonet-Fighting given by Maj. Campbell, Gordon Highlanders, assisted by C.S.M. Hirst of D Coy. In the afternoon B & D Coys fired Rapid Practice on the range & in the evening Battn. Hdqrs fired the same practice. Battn. football team played a match against 92nd F.A. at OFFOY and won by 2 goals to 1. Heavy rain stopped the game a little early.	4 E.D.
CANIZY	11.5.17		Parades were carried out in keeping with programme of training. In the afternoon Shooting matches took place between Coys for prizes and incidentally to evolve a team of 7 to be chosen to represent the battalion in the Brigade Competition held in the evening. In the latter the team consisted of C.S.M. Hirst, Pte. Hughes, Pte. Mowat, Sgt. Fleming, Cpl. Spence, Pte. Pullen and Pte. Chatham, and this was the 2nd KOYLI — the only other unit who sent a team — being the unit who practice 110 yds + 200 yds application and 15-sec Rapid (1 minute) at 300 yds. Our result was a win for battalion by 256 points against 248. Yes. Coy competitors resulted 1. D Coy, 2 A Coy, 3 Battn. Hdqrs, 4 C Coy, 5 B Coy.	4 E.D.

Army Form C. 2118

WAR DIARY
or
INTELLIGENCE SUMMARY
(Erase heading not required.)

Instructions regarding War Diaries and Intelligence Summaries are contained in F.S. Regs., Part II. and the Staff Manual respectively. Title Pages will be prepared in manuscript.

Place	Date	Hour	Summary of Events and Information	Remarks and references to Appendices
CANIZY	12.5.17		Parades were carried out in keeping with the programme of training. In the evening afternoon competitions were held on the range at 15yds Rapid (1 minute) at 300yds. The competitions were divided according to rank and mounted :— Officers 2/Lieut MacLolgan; W.O. and Sergts; C.S.M. West (37 points highest score in battalion); Corpls, Sgts MacAllister; Pters 2/Cpls, L/Cpl Watson.	A(E)
CANIZY	13.5.17		Church Parade was held at 8.30 a.m. In the evening a very successful event was held & received the patronage of several visiting staff officers.	A(E)
CANIZY	14.5.17		In the forenoon battalion carried out a scheme of attack on OFFOY. The movement was carried out by Brigade and scheme was submitted to the C.O. by Officers Commanding Coys. In the afternoon preparations were made for the battalion moving next day.	A(E)
CANIZY VOYENNES NESLE CURCHY	15.5.17		Reveille 2.30 a.m., breakfast 3.30 a.m. Battalion paraded at 4.30 a.m. and moved off to VOYENNES where it joined the other Brigade units. The route was through the north of NESLE and into CURCHY where battalion halted for the day. The village had met with the same fate as all others in the district and lay in a state of ruin. It also bore signs of a bombardment while the German military graves showed many men to have been killed in August 1916. Just outside the village, in a S.W. direction, an excellent open air bathing pond had been built (presumably by the enemy) and was taken advantage of by the battalion.	A(E)
CURCHY ROSIÈRES	16.5.17		Reveille 1.30 a.m., breakfast 2.30 a.m.; parade for inspection 3.30 a.m. Battalion moved off from CURCHY at 4 a.m. and joined Brigade line of march at PUZEAUX. The route passed through PUNCHY, HALLU, CHILLY, MAUCOURT to ROSIÈRES. Of these villages little or no description is possible beyond the fact that while some semblance of streets can be traced in MAUCOURT and also southward, CHILLY and HALLU are just masses of masonry debris literally peppered with shell craters. The state of the ground all over is No Man's Land and the enemy's old trenches form beyond doubt the strongest natural form of the ground. The ⋯ trenches on foot standing in and ⋯ should ⋯ the Brig. Gen. Blacklock. ROSIÈRES is a fairly big country town, but sparsely populated at present; the houses in the immediate front of ROSIÈRES, on the main road, Brigade ⋯ being the target of some ⋯ especially in the vicinity of the church.	A(E)

Army Form C. 2118

WAR DIARY
or
INTELLIGENCE SUMMARY
(Erase heading not required.)

Instructions regarding War Diaries and Intelligence Summaries are contained in F.S. Regs., Part II. and the Staff Manual respectively. Title Pages will be prepared in manuscript.

Place	Date	Hour	Summary of Events and Information	Remarks and references to Appendices
ROSIÈRES HANGARD	17.5.17		Reveille 2.15am; breakfast 3.15am; parade for inspection 4am. Battalion marched off in Brigade line of march and proceeded through SAIX, CAYEUX, IGNACOURT, + AUBERCOURT where a detour was made through DEMUIN in a SSW direction to crossroads on main AMIENS-ROYE road where Brigade marched past Div. Gen. Shute. Turning down DOMART road later in a northerly direction, battalion marched to HANGARD where it was billeted.	A.E.D.
HANGARD	18.5.17		The day was fully occupied with preparations and kit carried out cleaning and inspection parades. Work was commenced on Shooting Range at the SW end of the village and suitable sites were chosen immediately north of the village for battalion parade, bombing, and musketry ground. Leave to AMIENS was granted for Officers and NCOs in proportion of 5% of the former and 1% of the latter per day.	A.E.D.
HANGARD	19.5.17		Reveille 6.15am. Parades were carried out in keeping with programme of training (consisting of Close Order Drill, Bayonet Fighting, Bombing, Musketry and Physical Drill) A Bngde. Mess was opened in the Lodge-buildings at the Chateau.	A.E.D.
HANGARD	20.5.17		Church Parade was held at 9.30am. Inspection of kit was held by the CO in front of chateau to accept the two methods of laying out equipment and using in billets. C.O's formation to the rank of Lt. Colonel was confirmed on this day.	A.E.D.
HANGARD	21.5.17		Parades were carried out in keeping with programme of training. Work was continued on the Range and Bayonet Fighting Ground. 2 Football matches were played in the afternoon and one in the evening, all of them being in the first round of the platoon football tournament.	A.E.D.
HANGARD	22.5.17		Orders called for an early reveille, 4am., and route-march at 6am., but owing to a downpour of rain this was cancelled. During the day billet inspections and lectures were carried out. In the afternoon two football matches were played and bay. cross country running was commenced.	A.E.D.
HANGARD	23.5.17		Battalion route-march was held from 8 to 10am and thereafter parades in keeping with the programme of training were carried out. In the evening C Coy fired Jumping Practice on the Range.	A.E.D.

WAR DIARY or INTELLIGENCE SUMMARY

Army Form C. 2118

(Erase heading not required.)

Place	Date	Hour	Summary of Events and Information	Remarks and references to Appendices
HANGARD	24.5.17		Parades were carried out in keeping with the programme of training. Fired Grouping Practice on the Range and a Pool Target was run for practice and small money prizes. In the afternoon D Coy fired Grouping Practice on the Range and a Pool Target was run for practice and small money prizes.	A & P.
HANGARD	25.5.17		Parades were carried out in keeping with the programme of training. A but Sweater lectured to Officers and N.C.Os at DOMART on Musketry. In the afternoon A Coy fired Grouping Practice. Work was continued on improvements to the Range, completion of Bombing and Bayonet fighting Bat.	A & P.
HANGARD	26.5.17		Parades were carried out in keeping with the programme of training. B Coy fired Application Practice on the Range. A Coy bathed in the afternoon. A letter of regret was received from Genl. Birdwood on our leaving his command and wishes us success in our new Corps. General Birdwood relinquished command of Division to take our similar duties in the 19th Division.	A & P.
HANGARD	27.5.17		Church Parade was held at 9.30 a.m. Coys bathed in the afternoon. Inventation of battalion was completed on this day. In the evening a football match between the officers and sergeants, the former won by 2 goals to 1.	A & P.
HANGARD	28.5.17		Battalion route march was held in the forenoon and ordinary parades were carried out thereafter. Bathing was continued and Battalion Pool competition was fired on the range. Work of smartening the range was carried out in view of the prospective move from this area.	A & P.
HANGARD	29.5.17		Parades were carried out in keeping with the programme of training. Training store was packed and arranged to ANIENS by battalion transport which returned to HANGARD and attracted preparatory to moving north.	A & P.
HANGARD – VILLERS-BRETONNEUX	30.5.17	Reveille 4.30 a.m., Breakfast 5.30 a.m.	Battalion moved off from HANGARD at 6.55 a.m. and marched to VILLERS-BRETONNEUX, where transport hutted till such time as entrainment commenced. Equipment was overhauled and polished.	A & P.
VILLERS-BRETONNEUX	31.5.17	Reveille 9 a.m.	Parades were held under Coy arrangements wholly musketry parades were continued on the Miniature Target. Companies completed the cleaning of equipment. Battalion football team played entraining fatigue party for transport departing at 10.15 p.m. Battalion followed by 2 guns to 1. C.Coy found attacked by Cav. R.E. & was attacked by	A & P.

1875 Wt. W593/826 1,000,000 4/15 J.B.C. & A. A.D.S.S./Forms/C.2118. 2.19 44 Coy R.E.

17th S.B.H.L.I.

Vol 20

War Diary

1st – 30th June
1917.

No. 8

Army Form C. 2118

WAR DIARY
or
INTELLIGENCE SUMMARY
(Erase heading not required.)

Instructions regarding War Diaries and Intelligence Summaries are contained in F.S. Regs., Part II. and the Staff Manual respectively. Title Pages will be prepared in manuscript.

Place	Date	Hour	Summary of Events and Information	Remarks and references to Appendices
VILLERS-BRETONNEUX	1st and 2nd June 1917		Arrangements were completed for entraining and at 2-30 p.m. battalion marched to station and at 5-45 p.m. the train left the station. C Coy. commanded having been detailed as loading party for Brigade. The journey was through AMIENS, ABBEVILLE, ETAPLES, BOULOGNE, CALAIS, ST. OMER, HAZEBROUCK, to STEENBECQUE. Unfortunately a short halt in the nine means at ABBEVILLE owing to the train having away without warning while the battalion was parading in the station for tea. With only some 180 all ranks on board this train continued its journey and in due course arrived at STEENBECQUE. The other officers and men who were left, followed in spare two of the 2nd MANCHESTERS from which steamed into the station as our former train moved off. The accommodation was decidedly meagre and consisted of unoccupied floor space of open trucks provided for regimental transport waggons leaving the Train at HAZEBROUCK the shrouded party marched to STEENBECQUE. Their appearance causing much interest to the inhabitants owing to the difference of equipment, rifles & usual in many case parts of their uniform. At the latter station the first party was picked up, packs & equipment were donned and battalion moved to a field in LE PARC where breakfast was served and a halt made for 4 hours. At 3-30 p.m. marched off and travelling via LA RUE DE MORTS, MERVILLE, NEUF BERQUIN arrived at a small scattered hamlet in the DOULIEU area. The battalion was billeted. Echinc Parade was had in a field opposite battalion Hdqrs at 3 p.m. All Coy. officers reconnoitred the route to the line. Reinforcements joined battalion and consisted of nine Lieut. and J.M. MacKay and 29 O.R.	
DOULIEU	3.6.17		B battalion took part in Brigade concentration march to STEENWERCK. Work was continued on the 30 yds range and Stiffhee Targets were prepared for practice. Reinforcements of 42 O.R. joined the battalion.	
DOULIEU	4.6.17		Parades were held in keeping with programme of training. In the forenoon A Coy fired on the range and in the afternoon B Coy carried out musketry practice.	
DOULIEU	5.6.17		Parades were carried out in keeping with programme of training and two Coys fired on range. During several urgent orders were received referring to the proposed attack on MESSINES and battalion "stood to" ready to move at a moment's notice.	

WAR DIARY
or
INTELLIGENCE SUMMARY

(Erase heading not required.)

Army Form C. 2118

Place	Date	Hour	Summary of Events and Information	Remarks and references to Appendices
DOULIEU	7.6.17		Parade was carried out in keeping with programme of training; two coys. fired on the range. Post shooting was also carried on and work was commenced on new range at B Coys billet. During the afternoon and night the intense preparatory bombardment of MESSINES was heard and battalion "stood to".	R.
DOULIEU	8.6.17		Undue were received relieving battalion from "Stand to" and giving welcome news of the successful offensive at MESSINES. Work was carried out completing B Coys range and firing took place on both ranges. Maj. Inglis – late 1st Batt. H.L.I. – joined battalion.	R.
DOULIEU	9.6.17		Packs, which had been dumped on the 9th was received from 2 W/otron. Parade was carried out in keeping with the programme of training. Musketry practice and post shooting were continued on the ranges.	R.
DOULIEU	10.6.17		At lunch parade was held in field opposite Batt. Hedqs. at 9-30 a.m. Post shooting was carried out on the ranges.	R.
DOULIEU	11.6.17		Parade was carried out in keeping with programme of training. Musketry practice and post-shooting was continued on the ranges and special award of musketry instruction for N.C.O's was commenced. Battalion Junior Brigade route-march and thereafter carried out the usual parade of musketry, bayonet fighting, bombing and physical drill. Post shooting was continued on the ranges and the NCO's musketry classes were held as usual.	R.
DOULIEU	12.6.17		Parade was carried out in keeping with programme of training, use being made of Divisional Bombing School for the throwing of live bombs. Musketry instruction, post shooting and general practices were continued. In the evening battalion received orders for next days move and ranges and training grounds were closed up.	R.
DOULIEU ECKE	14.6.17		Battalion paraded at 6 a.m. and at 6-18 marched off. The march was through CAESTRE – ESTAIRES and a little south of COURONNE. Thence the road led through VIEUX-BERQUIN, STRAZEELE to CAESTRE where it struck off	R.

1875 Wt. W593/826 1,000,000 4/15 J.B.C. & A. A.D.S.S./Forms/C. 2118.

WAR DIARY
or
INTELLIGENCE SUMMARY

(Erase heading not required.)

Army Form C. 2118

Place	Date	Hour	Summary of Events and Information	Remarks and references to Appendices
DOULIEU EECKE	14.6.17 (contd)		Off in a N.E. direction finally crossing the railway and joining the easterly road between EECKE and STEENVOORDE in which area battalion was billeted. The march proved one of the most trying the Battalion has ever had and many men fell out suffering from the heat & of driving sun which shone with pitiless intensity all the way; to this must be added the difficulties of traversing several long ascents en route. The distance travelled was about 24 kilometres, and the time taken 6 hours.	
EECKE	15.6.17		At 10 a.m. inspection of Transport took place and at 11 a.m. Transport moved off for the second days journey. The remainder of battalion spent the day cleaning and kit inspection was held at night. Orders were received for next days move.	
EECKE MARDYCK	16.6.17		Battalion moved off from starting point at 5-25 a.m. and was met by motor charabancs which along the road running N.W. into WORMHOUDT and conveying started. The route was through STEENVOORDE thence to the west leading through BIERNE and along the main road to near BERGUES road at LA MAISON BLANCHE the buses travelled westward and along the bank of BOURBURG CANAL across the bridge and up to PETITE SYNTHE. Leaving the motor charabancs at the cross-roads between — marched to billets at MARDYCK.	
MARDYCK	17.6.17		Billet inspection was held at 9 a.m. and at 10-30 battalion paraded for church service. At stated times, with suitable intervals, Bugs. paraded for sea bathing.	
MARDYCK PETITE-SYNTHE	18.6.17		Brigade carried out manoeuvres in the shunt practising attack according to Divisional methods of formation. After the attack bathing was indulged in by all units. Battalion prepared to move into PETITE SYNTHE at 5 p.m. but owing to a sudden thunderstorm the move was delayed and Battn.	
PETITE-SYNTHE COXYDE	19.6.17		moved off at 6 p.m. arriving in billets at 7-30 p.m. At 12 noon Battalion moved off from PETITE SYNTHE and marched into DUNKIRK where it entrained. Travelling eastward along the Coast dunes Battalion reached COXYDE where it detrained and marched towards ZEEPAN into JEANNIOT CAMP where billeting accommodation had been arranged. In the —— a sing-song/dance battalion concert held in the camp concert hall	

Army Form C. 2118

WAR DIARY
or
INTELLIGENCE SUMMARY
(Erase heading not required.)

Instructions regarding War Diaries and Intelligence Summaries are contained in F. S. Regs., Part II. and the Staff Manual respectively. Title Pages will be prepared in manuscript.

Place	Date	Hour	Summary of Events and Information	Remarks and references to Appendices
COXYDE & CAMP KUHN	20.6.17	8.30 am	Battalion left JEANNIOT CAMP and moved eastward to CAMP KUHN near OOST DUNKERKE and took over the lines according to Brigade orders. Coys. carried out parades in keeping with the programme of training.	
OOST DUNKERKE (CAMP KUHN)	21.6.17		In the morning much aerial activity was observed, several German machines leaving crossed our lines. Coys. carried out parades in keeping with the programme of training. In the evening the enemy opened fire on the area around the camp and lastly on the east end of OOST DUNKERKE which was bombarded for some time with high explosive and shrapnel. Instructions were received authorising R.S. Maj. Kelly to take the rank of Hon. Lieut. and Quartermaster of the battalion.	
OOST DUNKERKE (CAMP KUHN)	22.6.17		Coys. carried out parades in keeping with programme of training. Brigade issued instructions forbidding the use of telephones in areas in advance of Brigade Hdqrs. Capt. W.W. M'Intee assumed the rank of Major on this date. C.Coy moved from the camp at 9 pm. to take up support position NEW NIEUPORT and by 11 pm the move was completed without mishap. Aerial activity was much less than aerial during the unfavourable atmospheric conditions.	
OOST DUNKERKE (CAMP KUHN)	23.6.17		Coys. carried out parades in keeping with the programme of training. In the early morning (2-45 am) Battalion received a Gas Alarm and within 10 minutes all personnel were on parade fully equipped and wearing Box Respirators. Aerial activity was again very prominent in both sides during the entire day.	
OOST DUNKERKE (CAMP KUHN)	24.6.17		6 Lunch parade was held at the camp at 9am. Aerial activity was much greater than usual during the entire day, while the German anti-aircraft batteries fired all day without success, one of the enemy machines was seen to be driven down by one of our airmen. The enemy machines arrived out of control. At 9 pm an advanced party left camp to arrange for taking over the line from 114th Brigade.	
OOST DUNKERKE & NIEUPORT (PETIT REDAN)	25.6.17		Coys. carried out inspections in battle order and a further advance party left for the trenches. In the evening battn. moved up towards OOST DUNKERKE and from thence direct to the road junction the camp. The route was through OOST DUNKERKE and by 9-30 pm the last Coy. was clear of the southern opening of which leads to NIEUPORT. Crossing the YSER at the N of NIEUPORT, Coys carried out the relief without incident. Battn. Hdqrs. were established at PETIT REDAN	

WAR DIARY or INTELLIGENCE SUMMARY

Army Form C. 2118

Instructions regarding War Diaries and Intelligence Summaries are contained in F.S. Regs., Part II. and the Staff Manual respectively. Title Pages will be prepared in manuscript.

(Erase heading not required.)

Place	Date	Hour	Summary of Events and Information	Remarks and references to Appendices
NIEUPORT (PETIT REDAN)	26.6.17		Battalion in the line, holding NOSE TRENCH, left of Divisional front and opposite LOMBARDZYDE. 1st Brigade of 1st Division on the left and 96th Brigade on the right; MOBLI was on the immediate left being right battalion of brigade front. 16th M.G.I were in support at NIEUPORT and XI BORDERS in reserve at NEW PARADE and NEW WALK. The whole of day around the signs for enemy activity and his heavy trench mortars bombarded our front line; at times this bombardment of great intensity and much havoc was wrought to the direct work which constitute the only protection the men have. Late in the day enemy artillery of heavy calibre played on a small part of the right coy front – from NOSE AVENUE to NOSE ALLEY – and the communication trenches leading there. This artillery fire was returned for nearly 2 hours and much damage was done to the line while 7 men were killed. 1 injured and 10 buried but safely dug out. Three enemy aeroplanes were seen to cross our lines but retired on being fired at by our anti-aircraft guns. Two of our machines crossed the enemy lines and reconned. Shot some time though repeatedly fired at by the German artillery. A + B Coys held the front line system with D Coy in support and C Coy in reserve. In the night time large working parties from C and D Coys of XI Batto and 3 Coy of XI Borders repaired the damage. Two patrols left our battalion in the line. Aerial activity was early in evening particularly on the part of the enemy. Three of his machines tried our lines and retired at their own time though heavily shelled by our anti-aircraft guns. One of our machines flew boldly over the enemy lines and by means of some wonderful loops and spiral dives eluded the intense enemy fire directed against it. The rest of the observation was even too timid and an extremely severe bombardment by heavy trench mortars, rifle grenades and shells was started on our first three lines. Though slackening a little, the bombardment did not stop till about mid day when our artillery retaliated. This retaliation did not silence the enemy activity and throughout the morning the minenwerfer of the day a light ah trench mortar activity continued and an occasional shell was fired into our lines. The casualties were 3 OR killed and 5 OR wounded. At night working parties were again busy and much of the damage was repaired. Two patrols left our lines and reconnoitred No Man's Land and enemy wire, returning safely at the appointed time	R W Hodgson Capt.
NIEUPORT (PETIT REDAN)	27.6.17			

Army Form C. 2118

WAR DIARY
or
INTELLIGENCE-SUMMARY
(Erase heading not required.)

Instructions regarding War Diaries and Intelligence Summaries are contained in F. S. Regs., Part II. and the Staff Manual respectively. Title Pages will be prepared in manuscript.

Place	Date	Hour	Summary of Events and Information	Remarks and references to Appendices
NIEUPORT (PETIT REDAN)	28.6.17		Battalion in the line. The night passed with the usual desultory fire from enemy machine guns but an artillery fire was heard until a sudden burst of great intensity opened on the right slightly beyond our brigade front. At the same time some rifle attention was delivered on our battalion lines. Arial darts and rifle grenades formed the greater part of the missiles though a battery of 77 m.m. seemed to be distributing its fire along our lines. Our own artillery replied vigorously and rifle but reception during their recuperation. A was relieved by C Coy. The former having received a decidedly hot reception during their recuperation. During the day artillery was much quieter than usual, presumed 77m.m. being sent over against a wide front. The pontoon bridge over the YSER became the target for most of the enemy's shelling of the back area. Arial observation was rather less than usual owing to the atmospheric conditions. At night working parties were again busy repairing and strengthening the trenches. Our patrols left our lines to type with any enemy patrol which might be seen. The casualties for the past 24 hours were lights than usual 1 Officer and 1 OR being killed and 1 officer and 3 OR wounded.	
NIEUPORT (PETIT REDAN)	29.6.17		Battalion in the line. Working parties in the evening and next day were constantly shelled during the early hours, the finding of light shells and distributed over a wide front. Though the shelling was not intense the resultant casualties were of fair proportions and mainly among the battalions providing the parties. From 5.30am till noon an intermittent fire was directed against NIEUPORT and the areas and bridges leading thereto while the further back areas received attention from heavy shells fired from the direction of MIDDLEKERK. 6 of the latter fell in the area of CAMP KUHN when battalion details and transport was stationed; no casualties resulted. Starting at 9.30 pm the VI BORDERS moved up onto the line and relieved us. The relief being completed without incident by 1 am. Battalion Headquarters were established in NEW PARADE.	NR 7
NIEUPORT (NEW PARADE)	30.6.17		Battalion at NEW PARADE as Brigade Reserve. During the day companies carried out drill and equipment. At night Battalion supplied working parties for the trenches. Enemy artillery paid some attention than usual to the OOST-DUNKERKE and NEW PARADE areas and many 5.9 in. H.E and shrapnel were directed against this Aerial activity was much below the usual.	R.7 R,

1875 W: W593/826 1,000,000 4/15 J.B.C. & A. A.D.S.S./Forms/C. 2118.

WO 21

CONFIDENTIAL

WAR DIARY.

FROM 1st July to 31st July, 1917

VOLUME 9.

R. .... 2nd. LIEUT,
Intelligence Officer, 17th. H.L.I.

WAR DIARY
or
INTELLIGENCE SUMMARY.

Army Form C. 2118.

Place	Date	Hour	Summary of Events and Information	Remarks and references to Appendices
	1st July		Battalion at NEW PARADE as Brigade Reserve. The night passed without incident till 2 a.m. when our guns opened up a fairly intense bombardment of the enemy line in front of the right Brigade. The fire ceased about 2.30 a.m. with little enemy retaliation. Companies rested during the day and inspection of dug-outs was like in the late afternoon. Enemy artillery was active throughout the day reaching great intensity from 4 p.m. till 6 p.m. on reserve lines. Working parties were supplied by the Battalion for night work in the trenches. A Battalion Orderly Room was held at 6 p.m.	H.D.
	2nd July		Battalion at NEW PARADE as Brigade Reserve. Enemy artillery was fairly active throughout the night on reserve lines and rears and lit up an intermittent bombardment all day. Hostile aircraft displayed marked activity and continued after dusk. Companies rested during the day and supplied work parties at night for the trenches.	
	3rd July		Battalion at NEW PARADE as Brigade Reserve. About 12.30 a.m. our guns opened a heavy bombardment of enemy's trenches opposite the Reserve and continued till dawn. At 9.20 a.m. two of our aeroplanes attacked and forced down an enemy machine and at 9.35 a.m. another enemy plane was brought down by one of our aircraft. Hostile artillery was less active and the evening was very quiet. Companies rested during the day and	H.D.

WAR DIARY or INTELLIGENCE SUMMARY.

Army Form C. 2118.

Place	Date	Hour	Summary of Events and Information	Remarks and references to Appendices
	3rd July (cont⁴)		supplied work parties for night work in the trenches.	M.N
	4th July		Battalion at NEW PARADE as Brigade Reserve. The night passed without incident. Hostile artillery and aircraft were normal throughout the day and in the evening artillery was exceptionally quiet. Companies rested during the day and at night relieved the 11th Border Regt in LOMBARTZYDE Left sub-sector. A & D Companies went into the front line, C to Grand Redan, and B into two platoons in the LAITRIERE, one in PETIT REDAN and one in 4th line. No. Division were on our left and 14th Brigade on our right with 2nd K.O.Y.L.I. on immediate right. The relief was carried out without incident.	
	5th July		Battalion in C. Left Sub Sector. At 12.15 a.m. a raiding party of the 11th Border Regt. entered the enemy's line opposite our Battalion front. They met with heavy resistance and retired under our own barrage. At 1.45 a.m. a raiding party of the 16th H.L.I. entered the enemy's trench opposite the right Battalion front under cover of our barrage. Two prisoners were taken but one had to be disposed of as he showed resistance. The enemy made a spirited reply and at 3.10 a.m. heavily bombarded the Brigade front with heavy artillery and mortars. Our artillery replied and at 4 a.m. hostile activity eased off. A & D Companies suffered casualties amounting	M.N

WAR DIARY
or
INTELLIGENCE SUMMARY.

(Erase heading not required.)

Army Form C. 2118.

Place	Date	Hour	Summary of Events and Information	Remarks and references to Appendices
	5th July (contd).		to 4 O.R. killed and 70 O.R. wounded. The day passed uneventfully, the enemy making no further attacks at retaliation. At night the 11th Border Regt. supplied work parties to improve the trenches. The transport bringing the rations was shelled on the road leading from POST DUNKERQUE to between NIEUPORT and NIEUPORT BAINS, 3 O.R. being evacuated. Two patrols left our lines about 11.15 p.m. to take possession of "No Man's Land". One enemy work party was encountered and dispersed by Lewis Gun fire. The Enemy showed greater vigilance afterwards.	
	6th July		Battalion in "C" Left Sub Sector. The night passed without incident and the enemy remained quiet until 9 a.m. when he opened a desultory fire on our trenches and reserve. Towards the afternoon he became increased and even sent up a light Lights. The enemy tank and HUTTIERS came in for special attention. Our lines retaliated and took one direct hit on a very high altitude. Casualties for the day amounted to 1 O.R. killed and 18 O.R. wounded.	R.D.
	7th July		Battalion in "C" LEFT SUB SECTOR. Two patrols left our lines about 12.30 a.m. and encountered and dispersed an enemy work party repairing their own trench. Aerial activity commenced at dawn and continued throughout the day, displaying great daring. Our tank mortars and artillery subjected the enemy lines to a heavy bombardment for about 20 minutes, commencing	R.D.

WAR DIARY
or
INTELLIGENCE SUMMARY.

(Erase heading not required.)

Army Form C. 2118.

Place	Date	Hour	Summary of Events and Information	Remarks and references to Appendices
	7th July (cont)	8.55 a.m.	The enemy retaliated heavily and his artillery continued a heavy bombardment throughout the day. The HUITRIEBE and NIEWPORT area was heavily bombarded by 8" howitzers being however MIDDLEKIRK direction. Fire slackened towards dusk and by 9 p.m. both fire had ceased. "C" Coy relieved "A" Coy in front line. A enemy to GRAND REDAN. Casualties for the day amounted to 2 O.R. killed and 7 O.R. wounded.	A-D
	8th July.		Battalion in "C" left SUB SECTOR. A hostile biff an bomb about 12:30 a.m. and leaving very destructive wounds of working on the escape two made at once by the got and were met with a fusilade of bombs and machine gun fire. Though defeated to met our long line they managed to reach our own lines without mishap. The remainder of the night passed quietly. 1 at at dawn both hostile artillery commenced a bombardment which continued heavily throughout the day. Enemy used 8" howitzers in great numbers and a 12" gun fired a depen rounds in the vicinity of NIEWPORT. The made use of gas shells occasionally throughout the bombardment. At night the 11th Border Regt. relieved us without mishap. Battalion continued working till night and at dawn proceeded to NEW PARADE and NEW WALK as Brigade Reserve.	A-D

WAR DIARY or INTELLIGENCE SUMMARY

Army Form C. 2118.

Place	Date	Hour	Summary of Events and Information	Remarks and references to Appendices
	9th July		Battalion at NEW PARADE as Brigade Reserve. The night passed without incident and at dawn both artillery shewed a slack line, the rear receiving marked attention. Confidence ruled during the day and supplied working parties to the line at night. About 11.30 p.m. our guns opened a heavy bombardment on to Burnon on our left front. The enemy making a strong reply. Casualties for the day amounted to 6 OR killed and 11 OR wounded.	
	10th July		Battalion at NEW PARADE as Brigade Reserve. The night passed very quietly and about 5 a.m. the enemy shewed a bombardment on all lines, reserve and rear. The bombardment at 4 hours a.m. heavier and soon reached an unprecedented pitch. The Burnon on our left was receiving it a little lower than us. Our guns were replying but the battle fire never slackened. At 10.20 a.m. the platoon of "9" Coy. moved into the PRESQUILE Alamo to support the running platoon of the Coy. which was already replying them. The enemy attacked his greatest efforts being made against the Burnon on our left and at 1.30 p.m. A & C Coys moved off to support the 11th Border Regt. who had sustained heavy casualties. The enemy were unable to cross the bridge — PUTNEY BRIDGE to the PETIT REDAN but were unable to cross the bridge	

WAR DIARY or INTELLIGENCE SUMMARY

Army Form C. 2118.

Place	Date	Hour	Summary of Events and Information	Remarks and references to Appendices
	10th July (con.)		to the GRAND REDAN. They then proceeded via the 16th H.L.I. Headquarters and moved into the 4th line, B on the left, A on the right. B Coy. had one platoon as flank guard on NOSE LANE from Lt. off. to 3rd line on the enemy had by this time carried the Redoubts of the 1st Division. Bombing patrols were put forward by A & B Coys to reconnoitre the 2nd line (NOSE SUPPORT) but were unable to do so as the enemy had laid a heavy barrage on it. So the enemy C Coy moved up by the same route and took up an extreme left of 4th line	R.D.
	11th July		Battalion in PRESQUILE defences and 4th LINE on approach to 11th Border Regt. Soon after midnight the bombardment slackened but the enemy kept out. in bursts of hurricane fire throughout the night. Our bombarding. established posts in the 2nd line and were relieved by the 16th Northumberland Fusiliers of the 96th Brigade and A & C Coys. withdrew to the GRAND REDAN and B Coy. to the PETIT REDAN. The day was fairly active the enemy keeping up a bombardment among other things a new kind were large number of gas shells the gas being a mixture of gas shells the gas being a mixture of shell had a very bad effect on the eyes. At night A, B & C Companies were relieved by the 15th H.L.I. and the 14th. Brigade and "B" Coy. by a Company of the 16th Northumberland Fusiliers. A hurricane bombardment fired during the relief and lasted about 30 minutes and patrols followed	

WAR DIARY
or
INTELLIGENCE SUMMARY.

Army Form C. 2118.

Place	Date	Hour	Summary of Events and Information	Remarks and references to Appendices
	11th July (con.)		by which slight hounds of heavy loss. The casualties in the action of the 10/11th amounted to: CAPT. E. DOBSON, killed and LIEUT. R.C. McCANKIE, 2/LT. R. WILSON, 2/LT. J. TALBOT, 2/LT. H.R. PEAT, 2/LT. A.R. PRIMROSE, 2/LT. K. REID and 2/LT. T.A. DICKIE wounded, 11 o.R. killed and 90 O.R. wounded.	M?
	12th July		BATTALION at JEAN BART CAMP, COXYDE. The Battalion arrived at the Camp of which some of which received a bombardment of 900 shells him NIEUPORT to OOST DUNKERQUE, 3 or 4 being wounded. Companies rested till the late afternoon when packs were drawn and cleaning up commenced. Battalion was put on one hours notice and orders issued that no one was to leave Camp.	A.D
	13th July.		BATTALION AT COXYDE as Divisional Reserve. The Commanding Officer, 2/LT. and 20 o.R. left on leave at 6 a.m. the large allotment causing great jubilation among the men. CAPT. G.R.S. PATERSON. M.C. assumed Command of the Battalion during the absence of the C.O. on leave. Orders for stand to as the S.O.S. signal had gone up from the line and the necessary arrangements were completed to ensure that movement could take place within 15 minutes of receiving instructions to proceed forward.	M.?

Army Form C. 2118.

WAR DIARY
or
INTELLIGENCE SUMMARY.
(Erase heading not required.)

Instructions regarding War Diaries and Intelligence Summaries are contained in F. S. Regs., Part II. and the Staff Manual respectively. Title pages will be prepared in manuscript.

Place	Date	Hour	Summary of Events and Information	Remarks and references to Appendices
	14th July.		Battalion at COXYDE as Divisional Reserve. The Battalion was on 15 minutes notice all night and in the morning word was received that the enemy had failed in an attack and that an alteration of area had led to the recovery of some of the ground lost on the 10th inst. Battalion was put on two hours notice in the afternoon. A hostile aeroplane flew over the Camp in the early morning and dropped three bombs in the South of the Camp. 6 companies and billets were inspected by the C.O. in the forenoon and the transport in the afternoon. The remainder of the day passed without incident.	A.D.
	15th July.		Battalion at COXYDE as Divisional Reserve. Church Parade and inspection of billets was held in the forenoon and preparation made for shifting to GHYVELDE area to-morrow. The men were confined about midnight.	A.D.
	16th July.		Battalion at COXYDE as Divisional Reserve. Hostile aircraft passed over the Camp during the night. Orders were received to proceed to POST DUNKERQUE to quickly work parties under the charge of the 257th Coy (Tunnelling) R.E. The move was completed in the early afternoon and the Battalion encamped in the R.E. Camp. Battalion Headquarters, D.H. Office and Transport being billeted in the village. C Coy supplied one Officer and "9" Coy, one Officer and 220 o.r. and 220 o.r. a.m. "9" Coy, commence fatigues. A & B Coys remained at the Camp supplying small parties for work at the R.E. Dump.	A.D.

Army Form C. 2118.

WAR DIARY
or
INTELLIGENCE SUMMARY.
(Erase heading not required.)

Instructions regarding War Diaries and Intelligence Summaries are contained in F. S. Regs., Part II. and the Staff Manual respectively. Title pages will be prepared in manuscript.

Place	Date	Hour	Summary of Events and Information	Remarks and references to Appendices
	17th July.		Battalion at OOST DUNKERQUE. A draft of 30 o.r. was ordered but only 28 o.r. arrived as 2 were absent when draft left the base. Plan of the elevation arrived at 10 p.m. The C.O. & M.O. inspected the draft in the evening. Orders were received that the Battalion was to proceed to the GUYVELDE area to relieve the 49th Brigade as being relieved by the 49th Division. Arrangements to meet on the 20th were made and a message of congratulation from the Corps Commander LIEUT. GENERAL SIR. J.P. DU CANE, K.C.B. was read on the parade that day in the NIEUPORT AREA.	R.1)
	18th July.		Battalion at OOST DUNKERQUE. The day passed without incident.	(R.1)
	19th July.		Battalion at OOST DUNKERQUE. In the early hours of the morning the outskirts of the village were heavily bombarded. The day passed quietly and orders were received that the two Companies in NIEUPORT would rejoin the Battalion at night. The Companies arrived safely about 11 p.m. Further orders arrived that the destination was changed to BRAY DUNES PLAGE and arrangements were made accordingly.	R.1)
	20th July.		Battalion at OOST DUNKERQUE. The Battalion moved off at 5 a.m. and proceeded via COXYDE, LA PANNE, ADINKERKE, BRAY DUNES to BRAY DUNES PLAGE. At ADINKERKE MAJOR J INGLIS joined and taking over Command	

WAR DIARY of INTELLIGENCE SUMMARY.

Army Form C. 2118.

Place	Date	Hour	Summary of Events and Information	Remarks and references to Appendices
	20th July (cont.)		of the Battalion. The Battalion bivouacked Batt. H.Q. being billeted in the village. The remainder of the day was spent cleaning up, the troops requiring a great deal of attention.	
	21st July.		Battalion at BRAY DUNES PLAGE. The C.O. Adjutant and Coy. Commanders reconnoitred the ground. French system of enemy defence in NIEUPORT area situated in the GHYVELDE area. The day was spent cleaning up and a Training Programme was issued stating the lines of training for specialists and parades for training xx.	
	22nd July.		Battalion at BRAY DUNES PLAGE. Church Parade was held and tub and tilter inspection made by arrangements. A range was started in the DUNES. A 2 B Coy supplying the party. Orders arrived that the Corps Commander would inspect the Brigade on the following day. Battalion being promoted full advantage was taken of this.	
	23rd July.		Battalion at BRAY DUNES PLAGE. Battalion was lined up along with the rest of the Brigade for inspection. At 9 am and at 9.30 the Corps General MAJOR GEN. SCHULTE arrived and inspected the Brigade. After his inspection he gave an address congratulating the Brigade on its fine fight against the enemy attack on the 10th inst. At 10.30 the Corps Commander arrived and inspected our platoons addressing the Brigade, congratulating the men on their clean and smart appearance and	

WAR DIARY
or
INTELLIGENCE SUMMARY

Place	Date	Hour	Summary of Events and Information	Remarks and references to Appendices
	23rd July (cont)		paid a high tribute to the fighting qualities displayed against the enemy at NIEUPORT. He afterwards presented the Military Medal Ribbons to Sgt. R. Mulligan C Coy, Pte. A. O. Tillet Lewis Gun Section, Pte. A. Forrest A Coy, Pte. C.L.W. Beckers Lewis Gun Section, Pte. J. Wilder B Coy. The Medals were also awarded to C.S.M. Farrell att. to Brigade.	R.D.
	24th July		Battalion at BRAY DUNES PLAGE. The Battalion carried out a tactical operation on the Dunes, which was an attack on a strong point by a Battalion supported by trench mortars Lewis Guns and with aeroplane observation. The scheme was successfully carried out and finished at 12.30 p.m. In the afternoon and evening work was continued on the range and on fatigue parties from all Companies.	R.D.
	25th July		Battalion at BRAY DUNES PLAGE. Owing to the bad weather the tactical operation arranged for the day had to be abandoned. Opportunity was taken instead of carrying out inspections, and orders were issued to move to COXYDE.	R.D.
	26th July		BATTALION at BRAY DUNES PLAGE. Battalion moved off at 7.10 a.m. and marched via LA PANNE to COXYDE where we relieved the 16th NORTHUMBERLAND FUSILIERS at CAMP JEANNOIT.	R.D.

Army Form C. 2118.

WAR DIARY
or
INTELLIGENCE SUMMARY.
(Erase heading not required.)

Instructions regarding War Diaries and Intelligence Summaries are contained in F.S. Regs., Part II. and the Staff Manual respectively. Title pages will be prepared in manuscript.

Place	Date	Hour	Summary of Events and Information	Remarks and references to Appendices
	27th July.		Battalion at CAMP JEANNOIT, COXYDE. Work parties were supplied for work at COXYDE and neighbourhood. 320 or being employed and at night a party of 200 or proceeded to NIEUPORT as a carrying party. The Brigade was put in Divisional Reserve to the 49th Division.	
	28th July.		Battalion at COXYDE. Work parties were supplied as on the day previous. The party which proceeded to the NIEUPORT AREA were heavily shelled with gas shell and H.E., but managed to return without mishap.	
	29th July.		Battalion at COXYDE. Work parties were supplied as on the 28th July. Word was received of a probable shift to COXYDE BAINS on Coast Defence but was cancelled later. Specialists underwent further training.	
	30th July.		Battalion at COXYDE. Small work parties were provided during the day and a party of 200 at night. Specialists underwent further training.	
	31st July.		Battalion at COXYDE. Preparations were started to set ready for Offensive Action, and specialists underwent further training. Word was received of the success of the 2nd & 5th Armies who started an offensive this morning.	

17/44/22

CONFIDENTIAL

WAR DIARY

From 1st August 1917
To   31st   "   "

Volume No 10

August 1917

J Inglis Lt Col
Commanding 17th (S) Bn H.L.I.

Army Form C. 2118.

WAR DIARY
or
INTELLIGENCE SUMMARY.
(Erase heading not required.)

Place	Date	Hour	Summary of Events and Information	Remarks and references to Appendices
August 1917	1st		Battalion at COXYDE. Preparations for action were completed and prepared for issue to the Companies.	R.D.
	2nd		Battalion at COXYDE. Orders were issued, and Companies instructed in the part they were to take in action. The weather conditions throughout the day were not of a favourable nature, and during the course of the evening official information was received from Brigade Headquarters postponing the offensive.	R.D.
	3rd		Battalion at COXYDE. — The bad weather continued overnight and during the following day, a strong blustering wind accompanied by continuous driving rain. The day passed without incident, the only notable feature, which was also marked on the two preceding days, being the silence of the enemy artillery, which had previously been heard both day and night.	R.D.
	4.		Battalion at COXYDE — The inclemency of the weather abating somewhat artillery activity was again resumed. Our guns shelled the enemy positions during the day and throughout the night a heavy bombardment was maintained. The enemy's retaliatory fire was comparatively weak. Further details were arranged for the proposed offensive	R.D.

WAR DIARY
or
INTELLIGENCE SUMMARY.

Army Form C. 2118.

Place	Date	Hour	Summary of Events and Information	Remarks and references to Appendices
August 1917	5th		Battalion at COXYDE. - The day was uneventful. Church Parade was held in the forenoon, and the return of good weather permitted of bathing, Companies being paraded to ST IDESGALDE PLAGE for this purpose.	n.r.
	6th		Battalion at COXYDE. - Physical training and drilling took place during the day and bathing was again indulged in. At night the Battalion and two other officers visited the line for reconnaissance purposes. The enemy resorted to shell during the evening and one shell landed in the camp, killing a horse. Our artillery retaliated heavily. In the early hours of the following morning a second shell landed in the camp, but no casualties resulted.	n.r.
	7th		Battalion at COXYDE. - Another day of relative calm was passed. Advantage was taken of the continued improvement in the weather conditions to have Company parades, and bathing was again permitted in the afternoon.	n.r.
	8th		Battalion at COXYDE. - The Battalion set out in the forenoon for the Dunes where further practice in the forms of attack was gone through. The remainder of the day passed quietly, but in the evening there was a renewal of enemy shelling in the vicinity of the camp.	n.r.

Place	Date	Hour	Summary of Events and Information	Remarks and references to Appendices
	August 1917	9th	Battalion at COXYDE. - During the early morning there was a continuance of the hostile shelling and, about 9am, an enemy airman flew over the Camp at a very low altitude. He was fired upon but succeeded in getting safely away. Word was sent to Company Commanders during the afternoon warning them that the Battalion would proceed to KUHN CAMP, OOST-DUNKERKE, the following forenoon to relieve the 16th R.S.F. A scheme for night-work was put forward and issued to Company Commanders, and orders were sent out conveying instructions as to the steps to be taken in the event of further hostile shelling during the night.	
		10½	Battalion at KUHN CAMP. - The Battalion proceeded to OOST-DUNKERKE, no mishaps, taking over billets from the 16th R.S.F. Orders were issued regarding procedure in the event of enemy shelling in the new camp and Gas Guards were detailed for duty. Shelling occurred during the night, but none of the shells landed within the Camp area. A football team was chosen to meet a team representing the Battalion. A football team was selected by the 9th H.L.I. (the Glasgow Highlanders) at GHYVELDE, on the following day, and arrangements	K.P. K.P.

WAR DIARY
or
INTELLIGENCE SUMMARY.

Army Form C. 2118.

Place	Date	Hour	Summary of Events and Information	Remarks and references to Appendices
August 1917		10th cont.	regarding leave and transport for men going to see the match was carried through.	R.D.
		11th	Battalion at KUHN CAMP. — The men were paid out during the fore-noon, and later, parties from the different Companies left for the football match at GHYVELDE, the C.O., the Adjutant, and several other officers also attending. Showery weather conditions prevailed during the game, and after some interesting play, the Glasgow Highlanders team proved too strong for our own eleven, scoring a well-merited victory by 4 goals to 0.	R.D.
		12th	Battalion at KUHN CAMP. — Divine Services were held in the forenoon for different denominations. Arrangements were made for working parties to proceed on night work on the YELLOW LINE. Sky parties left in the evening and returned about 3 a.m., when two casualties were reported :— 2nd Lieut. W.L. Thomson, and one O.R., both wounded. During the day, hostile shelling occurred in the vicinity of the camp, and this continued at night, and during the early hours of the following morning, enemy aerial activity also being marked.	R.D.

WAR DIARY
or
INTELLIGENCE SUMMARY.

Army Form C. 2118.

Place	Date	Hour	Summary of Events and Information	Remarks and references to Appendices
August 1917		13th	Battalion at KUHN CAMP. Companies paraded in the forenoon, and were marched to the Baths at COXYDE, those after ablutions being received a change of clothing. Bot Respirator Drills were gone during the day. The enemy intermittently shelled the vicinity of the Camp. Working parties again left in the evening the continue work on the YELLOW LINE. On the return of the parties casualties were reported - 2 O.R. wounded.	M.R.
		14th	Battalion at KUHN CAMP. Intimation was received that the Battalion would vacate KUHN CAMP (renamed QUEENSLAND CAMP), on the following day and proceed to the billets previously occupied by them at BRAY DUNES. Company Commanders were informed, and preparations were begun in readiness for the departure. Working parties were sent out at night. There was an absence of enemy shelling during the day and the night was also quiet.	M.R.
		15th	Battalion at BRAY DUNES CAMP. - The Battalion paraded about 10a.m. and left QUEENSLAND CAMP for BRAY DUNES, the vacated billets being taken over by the 20th Royal Fusiliers, 33rd Division.	M.R

WAR DIARY
INTELLIGENCE SUMMARY.
(Erase heading not required).

Army Form C. 2118.

Place	Date	Hour	Summary of Events and Information	Remarks and references to Appendices
	August 1917 15th Sept.		The route followed was from OOST-DUNKERKE — COXYDE — LA PANNE — BRAY DUNES to BRAY DUNES PLAGE. The march being accomplished in excellent time.	n.a.
		16th	Battalion at BRAY DUNES PLAGE. The day was spent in a thorough cleaning up after the previous day's march, and Companies were paraded for inspection. Preparations were begun for Battalion Sports to be held on 23rd and 24th August.	n.a.
		17th	Battalion at BRAY DUNES CAMP. Work was continued on lines similar to those of the previous day, Companies being paraded on the ground at BRAY DUNES Satin for inspection and inspection in Battalion Drill. In this connection a training programme was drawn up for issue to Companies, detailing daily periods of training to be followed while the Battalion remained out of the line. Orders were received that the Battalion would proceed to D. Camp, GHYVELDE, on the following day.	n.a.
		18th	Battalion at GHYVELDE — The Battalion marched to GHYVELDE as per arrangement, Companies taking over tents vacated by the Queen's Own, West Surrey. The rest of the day was passed quietly.	n.a.

WAR DIARY
INTELLIGENCE SUMMARY.

Army Form C. 2118.

Place	Date	Hour	Summary of Events and Information	Remarks and references to Appendices
	August 1917			
	19th		Battalion at GHYVELDE. — An immediate start was made with the training programme previously drawn up, full advantage being taken of the nature and situation of the new ground for this purpose. The day began with inspections of the lines and thereafter Companies were drilled by platoons and squads in general infantry work, the use of arms etc.	n.s.
	20th		Battalion at GHYVELDE. — Training was continued on similar lines and a start was made in connection with the Guard Mounting Competition inaugurated by the Commanding Officer with the object of improving the efficiency of the Battalion guards. Final arrangements were also made regarding the Battalion Sports Day.	n.s.
	21st		Battalion at GHYVELDE. A working party, under 2nd Lieut. A.D.Sinclair was detailed for duty and left camp early in the morning. The forenoon was occupied with inspections and drill, and in the afternoon the Commanding Officer inspected the first detail of the Guard Mounting Competition, D.Company – No 13 Platoon – being adjudicated the best guard of the day.	n.s.

WAR DIARY
INTELLIGENCE SUMMARY.

Place	Date	Hour	Summary of Events and Information	Remarks and references to Appendices
August 1917	22nd		Battalion at GHYVELDE. — Arrangements were made for firing practice on the range at BRAY DUNES, but this had to be abandoned owing to the XV Corps School taking over the range. Companies went on with training and were dismissed at 12 noon.	n.r.
	23rd		Battalion at GHYVELDE. — During the forenoon Companies had physical drill and men were detailed to arrange the course for the Battalion Sports. The Sports began at 11 o'clock under unpromising weather conditions, but as the day proceeded brilliant sunshine prevailed. Numerous events were run off before a large number of spectators. Arrangements had been made for the rationing of the men on the field, and tea, sandwiches, cakes, and biscuits were supplied.	n.r.
	24th		Battalion at GHYVELDE. The second day of the Battalion Sports opened with more promise. A larger number of guests and spectators attended, and including many Colonial officers, and the various events were keenly contested. Both by our own men and the entrants from other Battalions. As on the preceding day the rationing arrangements were successfully carried out. The	

Army Form C. 2118.

WAR DIARY
INTELLIGENCE SUMMARY.

Instructions regarding War Diaries and Intelligence Summaries are contained in F. S. Regs., Part II. and the Staff Manual respectively. Title pages will be prepared in manuscript.

Place	Date	Hour	Summary of Events and Information	Remarks and references to Appendices
August 1917	24th cont		prizes were presented at the conclusion of the Sports by two of the lady guests.	n.d
	25th		Battalion at GHYVELDE. - The Brigade Sports, which followed those of the Battalion, took place on the Saturday at GHYVELDE, under ideal conditions. The entries were numerous, but as the ground had been laid out in different sectors it was possible to have several events run off simultaneously. As on the previous day, the Battalion representatives made a very creditable showing, winning numerous prizes.	n.d
	26th		Battalion at GHYVELDE. - Church parades were the principal feature of the day, the Presbyterian Service being conducted in Camp by the Rev. Dr. Pitman of Edinburgh. Dr. Pitman delivered a very impressive address to the men which was heard with the closest attention. The remainder of the day was passed quietly. At night intimation was received that the Battalion was to proceed to the Forward Area on the following day, and arrangements were immediately made for carrying out the move.	n.d

Army Form C. 2118.

WAR DIARY
or
INTELLIGENCE SUMMARY.
(Erase heading not required.)

Place	Date	Hour	Summary of Events and Information	Remarks and references to Appendices
August 1917	27th		Battalion at COXYDE. — The Battalion left GHYVELDE in the forenoon, and proceeded along the beach to COXYDE, where the night was passed.	10.15
	28th		Battalion at Oost-DUNKERKE. — The move forward was continued, the Battalion leaving COXYDE for OOST-DUNKERKE on the morning of the 28th. Temporary quarters were occupied in QUEENSLAND CAMP. In the evening Companies left for the line to take over positions in the St GEORGES Sector from the 2nd A.S.L.I. The move was carried through without incident, A and B. Companies going into the front lines, with C Company at Nieuport, and D. Coy's remaining at Oost-DUNKERKE. Battalion Headquarters were established at the BRICQUETERIE. The enemy kept up a constant shelling of Nieuport during the night, but left the line untouched.	10.77
	29th		Battalion in the LINE. — The day was passed quietly the enemy continuing to direct his shelling in the direction of Nieuport. The weather was very wet, rain falling heavily and rendering the conditions of the broken down trenches very dangerous and difficult to occupy. At night, a change was made in the	

Army Form C. 2118.

WAR DIARY
of
INTELLIGENCE SUMMARY.
(Erase heading not required.)

Place	Date	Hour	Summary of Events and Information	Remarks and references to Appendices
	Aug 20th/1917	29th cont	disposition of companies. Battalion Headquarters moved to billets in the SARDINERIE, NIEUPORT, occupied by C. Company. H.Q. La Briquêterie was taken over by B. Coy. The shelling of Nieuport continued all night.	I.R.
		30th	Battalion at in the LINE. - Intimation was received during the forenoon that the enemy was shelling our front line. The Defence Scheme, detailing the dispositions of the various Companies and their duties in the LINE, was drawn up by the Commanding Officer and issued to all concerned. Casualty returns received from Companies during the day showed only 1 O.R. wounded (shock). Intelligence reports were received by the Commanding Officer and arrangements were made for carrying out patrol work and line fatigues during the night.	n.r.
		31st	Battalion in the Line. Shelling continued overnight, but no further casualties were reported. Reports on patrol work were received in the early morning and Company Commanders were met by the Commanding Officer at the BRICQUETERIE in the afternoon.	n.r.

17 HLI
Vol 23

WAR DIARY.

From September 1 to September 30, 1917.

Volume No 11

Oct. 1, 1917.

T.B.Morton. Major.
Commanding 17th Sr. H.L.I.

Army Form C. 2118.

WAR DIARY
or
INTELLIGENCE SUMMARY.
(Erase heading not required.)

Place	Date	Hour	Summary of Events and Information	Remarks and references to Appendices
September	1. 1917		Battalion in the Line. - A patrol went out during the night to reconnoitre ROODE POORT FARM and POLDER FARM. They encountered some enemy opposition but returned to our lines without suffering any casualties, having obtained valuable information regarding the area reconnoitred. Overnight the enemy artillery kept up a heavy and incessant shelling of NIEUPORT, our guns retaliating with equal intensity. Casualties for the day were slight, only 2 O.R. being reported wounded by shell fire. The enemy shelling during the day-time was less marked. NIEUPORT was shelled intermittently and some shelling was also reported from our third line. A third casualty occurred, making a total for the 24 hours of 3 O.R. wounded. Enemy aerial activity was slight.	R.P.
"	2. 1917		Battalion in the Line. - Further patrol work was carried out during the early hours of the morning. A working party of 28 O.R. and 2 N.C.O.s. under 2nd. Lieut. Nicholson reported at Battalion H.Q. in the forenoon for service with the 256th Tunnelling Coy. One of the party sustained a slight shrapnel	R.P.

Army Form C. 2118.

WAR DIARY = Sheet 2.
INTELLIGENCE SUMMARY.
(Erase heading not required).

Place	Date	Hour	Summary of Events and Information	Remarks and references to Appendices
September	2. contd.		wound whilst waiting outside Batt. H.Q. (the SARDINERIE) and was sent to hospital. A protective S.O.S. Barrage was opened at 11.30 P.M. on the enemy's front line. All 18 'pdrs in S.O.S. lines between GELEIDE BROOK and the NIEUWLAND POLDER were engaged in this, 3 rounds per gun per minute being fired. The barrage lifted at 3 minute intervals 300 yards forward to LAZY TRENCH — LOVERS' WALK — BAMBURGH WALK. Howitzer battery work was continued during the barrage. The enemy did not retaliate to any appreciable extent but maintained the usual shelling of NIEUPORT all day, and during the night	R.?
Sept.	3.	1917.	Battalion in the Line. — Patrols again went out during the night to reconnoitre the vicinity of RODDE POORT FARM. A report submitted by O.C. "C" Company showed that the Patrol carried through some very daring work, obtaining information of considerable value. 2nd Lieutenant Fuller and Corporal Wilson "C" Company waded across the swamp approaches to the farm. Coming to a point where the water was two feet deep for wading, Corporal Wilson swam across and, on reaching ground, crawled in the direction of the enemy's line, finding another stretch of water, but no tracks of any kind. The ground between this point	R.?

WAR DIARY — Sheet 3.
INTELLIGENCE SUMMARY.

Army Form C. 2118.

Place	Date	Hour	Summary of Events and Information	Remarks and references to Appendices
Sept.	3.	Contd.	and the enemy lines were found to be waterlogged and impassable for troops. Lepore Wilson swam back to the point where the patrol had been covering his movements, and selecting another point, again swam across the canal to examine ground to the East, opposite the turn buildings. Here also, the ground was found to be very marshy, and no track could be found. One officer and 3 men then crossed the canal to the Eastern side to reconnoitre ground that which was found to be in a fairly good condition. Becoming aware which they were unable to bridge. They returned. An enemy patrol wiring party was observed about 300 yards distant and a patrol of 5 of the enemy was also seen about 200 yards South moving towards the working party, but no action could be taken against them as our patrol was unable to cross the ditch of water between them and the enemy. Shelling continued at intervals during the day, and the atmosphere being very clear, aerial observation was again carried out. Companies were warned during the afternoon	

WAR DIARY - SHEET 4.

INTELLIGENCE SUMMARY.

Place	Date	Hour	Summary of Events and Information	Remarks and references to Appendices
Sept.	3. cont.		That relief moved take place at night. An Operation Order detailing the scheme of relief was prepared by the Commanding Officer and issued to all concerned. The Battalion was relieved by the 11th Border Regiment and proceeded to billets at OOST-DUNKERKE, relief being completed without incident.	
	September 4, 1917		Battalion at QUEENSLAND CAMP. — Billets in QUEENSLAND CAMP were reoccupied by the Battalion, a hot meal being supplied to the men on arrival. The early part of the day was uneventful, being mainly occupied with training. In the afternoon, however, about 2 P.M. the enemy shelled the CAMP causing several casualties. A hut occupied by B. Company was struck. Two Sergeants who were in the hut at the time were killed and one sergeant and 3 O.R. seriously wounded. One O.R. belonging to "H" Company was also killed. The total casualties being — Killed 3; wounded 4. ~~...~~ ~~...~~ ~~...~~ ~~...~~ ~~...~~ Battalion ~~...~~ billets. In the evening "B" Company were moved to billets in WULPEN. A working party 200 strong	M.7.

WAR DIARY SHEET 5.
INTELLIGENCE SUMMARY.

Army Form C. 2118.

Place	Date	Hour	Summary of Events and Information	Remarks and references to Appendices
	Sept. 4. contd		Left Camp in the evening for duty on the YSER LINE, NIEUPORT under the R.E. There was no further shelling of the Camp during the night.	R.D.
	Sept. 5. 1917.		Battalion at QUEENSLAND CAMP. — In view of the probable further shelling of the Camp, training routine was confined as much as feasible. Arrangements were, however, made for the training of a special guard for Brigade. Considerable aerial activity was observed from the Camp in the afternoon. Half in the day an Operation Order was issued intimating that the remaining Companies in Camp, with the exception of Q.M. Stores and the Transport would move at night to Billets in WULPEN, south of the Canal. Shortly before starting time the enemy again shelled the Camp. Advantage was taken of the shelling-positions previously selected, and on this occasion no casualties were recorded. Companies moved off as per Order to the new Billets at WULPEN and on arrival strict orders were issued regarding movement outside Billets in the day-time. All ranks were warned against moving about	R.D.

WAR DIARY SHEET 6.
INTELLIGENCE SUMMARY

Army Form C. 2118.

Place	Date	Hour	Summary of Events and Information	Remarks and references to Appendices
Sept.	5 contd.		about on the main road in front of billets, advantage to be taken of the cover afforded by peats to the rear. It was not considered advisable to proceed with training in these circumstances as this area, for the greater part, was under enemy balloon observation. A working party, which left for duty at night met with casualties near ALBERT BRIDGE, 2nd Lieut. M. Yetter being severely wounded (since dead); one O.R. killed, and 5 O.R. wounded.	R.
	September 6, 1917.		Battalion at WULPEN.— The Bayonet fighting and Physical training course for N.C.O.s under a special instructor was resumed outside the training ground having been found to near of the billets. The training of the special guard was also continued. Nothing unusual occurred during the day, and at night working parties left for the Rine, to engage, under the supervision of Special Coys, R.E. in the preliminary arrangements for a proposed gas projector stores mortar attack on the enemy on the nights 7/8th and 8/9th.	R.
	September 7, 1917.		Battalion at WULPEN.— The day was passed quietly, the men being permitted to rest as much as possible. Working parties left	R.

WAR DIARY SHEET. 7.
INTELLIGENCE SUMMARY.

Army Form C. 2118.

Place	Date	Hour	Summary of Events and Information	Remarks and references to Appendices
	Sept. 7 contd		as usual in the evening and further casualties occurred one Sergeant and 2 O.R. being wounded by shell fire. The wind being unfavourable that night, the proposed gas attack was postponed.	R.O.
	September 8, 1917.		Battalion at WULPEN. — Another quiet day was passed. At night the projected gas attack was successfully carried through. The enemy retaliated with heavy machine gun fire, and a considerable number of white lights were seen to go up from his lines, but no heavy shelling followed. There were signs of a general slackening of artillery activity though shelling of the back areas continued.	R.O.
	September 9, 1917.		Battalion at WULPEN. — Divine Services for Roman Catholics were held in the forenoon in WULPEN Church and bathing took place at the baths near the canal, clean changes of under-clothing being issued to the men. At night the Battalion again moved forward taking over the line held by the 16th H.L.I. in the Right Sub-sector, ST. GEORGES SECTOR, C. Coy went to positions on the Right; D. Coy to the Left, with B. Coy in Support and A. Coy remaining in Reserve at GROOTE LABEUR Farm.	R.O.

Army Form C. 2118.

WAR DIARY; SHEET 9.
of
INTELLIGENCE SUMMARY.
(Erase heading not required).

Instructions regarding War Diaries and Intelligence Summaries are contained in F. S. Regs., Part II. and the Staff Manual respectively. Title pages will be prepared in manuscript.

Place	Date	Hour	Summary of Events and Information	Remarks and references to Appendices
	Sept. 11	Contd.	Patrol were unable to proceed further without being seen by the enemy. They lay down to observe his line but no movement was noticed. The patrol returned safely to our line. Nothing unusual occurred during the day except that the enemy aerial activity was again noticeable. Aircraft flew over our positions, but on every occasion they were met with heavy machine gun fire and forced to retire. At night a raid on the enemy's line was carried out by the Brigade on our left, the consequent artillery and machine gun fire being somewhat heavy.	
Battalion in the Line.	Sept. 12. 1917.		Enemy aerial activity was again prominent throughout the day, planes crossing our lines on several occasions. During the afternoon our own patrols were active, the enemy retaliating than slackening off. Artillery fire continued all day. Shelling was not severe, but several light shells fell in the vicinity of B. Bay. Headquarters. During the forenoon Brigadier-General Blacklock D.S.O., visited the line and expressed satisfaction with the general appearance and spirit of the men.	

WAR DIARY: SHEET 8.

Army Form C. 2118.

Place	Date	Hour	Summary of Events and Information	Remarks and references to Appendices
Sept.	9. contd.		The relief move was completed without incident. A patrol whose detailing the work to be done each night were drawn up, and a patrol went out at night in accordance with the scheme. The wind being unfavourable, gas were not projected over the enemy's lines, as proposed, that night.	R.D.
September	10. 1917.		Battalion in the Line. — The enemy remained comparatively quiet throughout the day though our lines were shelled at intervals. No casualties occurred. Hostile aerial activity was shown; an enemy airman flying low over our lines during the forenoon. At night we fired a number of gas shells in the direction of the enemy lines. The situation overnight continued normal.	R.D.
September	11, 1917.		Battalion in the Line. — A patrol of 2 N.C.Os. who went out in the early morning to reconnoitre the POLDERLEED in the direction of VENICE POST, discovered a dry-track 5'15"x 6 ft. broad about halfway to the POLDERLEED. This track could take infantry in fours. Tracings of footprints leading to and from this point were also observed. The	R.D.

WAR DIARY SHEET OF
INTELLIGENCE SUMMARY.

Army Form C. 2118.

Instructions regarding War Diaries and Intelligence Summaries are contained in F. S. Regs., Part II. and the Staff Manual respectively. Title pages will be prepared in manuscript.

Place	Date	Hour	Summary of Events and Information	Remarks and references to Appendices
Sept.	12. contd.		men, particularly those composing the guards on duty. Orders were issued with a view to minimising the traffic along the duck-walk from B. Coy H.Q. to Battalion H.Q., part of which the enemy had shelled. Patrol work was carried out at night with a view to ascertaining the nature of suspected operations carried on by the enemy in the vicinity of VENICE POST. The patrol reported in about midnight. Additional precautions therefore taken against the possibility of an enemy gun attack, but nothing occurred during the night.	
September 13. 1917.			Battalion in the Line.— The Third Anniversary of the forming of the Battalion was spent in the trenches. A telegram was received from the Brigadier and a reply was sent reciprocating the General's good wishes. Enemy aerial activity was again very noticeable during the day and there was a continuance of hostile shelling. Daylight patrol work was continued with successful results. At night a further Stokes mortar gas attack was directed against the enemy's lines. Casualties for the day were = 2 O.R. wounded.	K.17

WAR DIARY
INTELLIGENCE SUMMARY.

Army Form C. 2118.

Place	Date	Hour	Summary of Events and Information	Remarks and references to Appendices
	September 14, 1917.		Battalion in the Line. — A visit was paid in the forenoon by the Divisional Commander. Enemy aerial activity and the continued shelling of NIEUPORT were features of the day. The enemy were shelling GROOTE LABEUR farm. A report was received from O.C. "A" Company. Two casualties were reported from this quarter, but 3 O.R. were sent down from the line wounded during the day. Little patrol work was organised for the night, one patrol going out from NAMELESS HOUSE to reconnoitre the POLDER and another proceeding from NICE POST to report on the condition of NO MAN'S LAND.	R.O.
	September 15, 1917.		Battalion in the Line. — Companies were warned that the Battalion would be relieved that night by the 11th Border Regiment, the scheme of relief being that A and B.C. Companies would, and H.Q. would proceed to Billets in OOST-DUNKERKE and D. Coy to WELLINGTON CAMP. The day passed quietly through reports of shelling were received from C. Coy. Enemy airmen were again active over our lines but on every visit they were met with heavy machine gun fire and driven off. Relief was completed at night without incident.	R.O.

Army Form C. 2118.

WAR DIARY ; SHEET 12.
~~INTELLIGENCE SUMMARY~~

(Erase heading not required)

Instructions regarding War Diaries and Intelligence Summaries are contained in F. S. Regs., Part II. and the Staff Manual respectively. Title pages will be prepared in manuscript.

Place	Date	Hour	Summary of Events and Information	Remarks and references to Appendices
	September 16, 1917		Battalion at OOST-DUNKERKE. — The enemy shelled WELLINGTON CAMP during the forenoon, creating some nervousness but causing no casualties. Details from COXYDE rejoined the Battalion and the training of the special guard was resumed. The pipe band is considerably augmented, also resumed practice. There was not considered advisable to carry on with ordinary routine, drilling, etc., but Companies supplied working parties for night work in the line. There was some shelling of OOST-DUNKERKE and its environs all night.	R.R.
	September 17, 1917		Battalion at OOST-DUNKERKE. — Nothing of particular importance occurred during the day. There was again some shelling but little material damage resulted. Fatigue Parties as left for work in the line at night had to return owing to transport difficulties.	R.R.
	September 18, 1917		Battalion at OOST-DUNKERKE. — The day was again uneventful except for the usual shelling. The village, however, was coming under range of the enemy's guns. Work was again carried out at night.	R.R.

Army Form C. 2118.

WAR DIARY: SHEET. 13.
of
INTELLIGENCE SUMMARY.
(Erase heading not required.)

Place	Date	Hour	Summary of Events and Information	Remarks and references to Appendices
September 19, 1917.			Battalion at OOST DUNKERKE. – Another uneventful day was passed. Training being carried on, as far as possible in the circumstances, for the special guard, and for observers and snipers. During the day the Statement of Sgt. Phillips (R.W.F.) - prisoner of war in Germany - which was obtained from captured German documents, was read out to all ranks. Intimation was received that 4 O.R. had been wounded at WELLINGTON CAMP by shell fire in the morning. At night orders were (re)received and wired to all concerned detailing the taking over by the Battalion of Billets in COXYDE (CANADA CAMP), the 5/6th ROYAL SCOTS relieving. There was again some shelling of the village by the enemy at night, but relief was completed safely.	A.D.
September 20, 1917.			Battalion at COXYDE. – The Battalion left OOST-DUNKERKE for COXYDE in the evening, relief being completed without incident. Billets were occupied in CANADA CAMP. The night was quiet, none of the shelling of the Camp, previously experienced, taking place.	A.D.
September 21, 1917.			Battalion at COXYDE. Nothing of special note occurred during the day, but at night word was received that the Battalion would prepare	A.D.

WAR DIARY; SHEET 14.

INTELLIGENCE SUMMARY.

Army Form C. 2118.

Place	Date	Hour	Summary of Events and Information	Remarks and references to Appendices
Sept. 2	cont^d.		to move the following day to BRAY DUNES the Brigade moving from the forward Area to be taken over by "A" Infantry Brigade, 42nd Division Operation Orders detailing the scheme of the move were issued and arrangements made to have it carried out on the morrow.	R.P.
	September 22, 1917.		Battalion at BRAY DUNES. — The relief was effected during the afternoon "A" Infantry Brigade arriving at COXYDE by 'bus. The Battalion set out for BRAY DUNES where Billets were taken over in the village. Arrangements were made for a general cleaning up and orders regarding discipline and routine were forwarded to Companies. In addition to the Battalion Quarter Guard a special guard was detailed for the Corps Ordnance Dump at BRAY DUNES. Arrangements were also made for the holding of divine service on the following day (Sunday) and Companies were instructed to continue with the cleaning up of arms and equipments.	R.P.
	September 23, 1917.		Battalion at BRAY DUNES. — Divine Service was held in the forenoon, and for the rest of the day the men were off duty. In the afternoon	R.P.

Army Form C. 2118.

WAR DIARY SHEET 15
INTELLIGENCE SUMMARY

Place	Date	Hour	Summary of Events and Information	Remarks and references to Appendices
	Sept 23 cont'd		word was received that the Battalion would again move forward and retake over the Billets in CANADA CAMP which they had vacated the day previous. This change in plans necessitated arrangements for the move forward being at once made. This was done & a Warning Order being issued which was followed later by the Operation Order.	I.O.
"	September 24, 1917		Battalion Recons BRAY DUNES.- Final arrangements for the move were completed and the Battalion was ready to proceed at 12 noon. Companies set out about an hour and a half later, the route taken being along the sands via LA PANNE - ST IDESBALDE - COXYDE. The march discipline was extremely good in spite of the heat and the somewhat heavy nature of the ground. Some distance off LA PANNE the Battalion was halted and sea-bathing was permitted, the sea little were re-occupied about 6 p.m. and evenes for routine were prepared, the usual anti-gas and aircraft precautions being taken. Notices were exhibited in Battalion Orders that the "Pedlars" Entertainers had been booked to give an performance for the men of the Battalion on the following evening.	I.O.?

WAR DIARY: SHEET 16

INTELLIGENCE SUMMARY.

Army Form C. 2118.

Place	Date	Hour	Summary of Events and Information	Remarks and references to Appendices
Battalion at COXYDE.	September 25, 1917.		During the day Companies were paraded and marched to the Baths at COXYDE where on completion of bathing clean underclothing was supplied to the men. This day passed quietly, and in the evening Officers and men attended the "Pedlar" Performance in the Cinema Tent. About midnight the enemy shelled the area of the Camp, but no casualties were reported in our lines.	R.D.
Battalion at COXYDE.	September 26, 1917.		There was a resumption of the shelling during the day but no damage was done. Otherwise there was nothing to record.	R.D.
Battalion at COXYDE.	September 27, 1917.		Further shelling occurred overnight, but the day was quiet. Intimation was received that the Battalion would move forward on the night of the 28/29th to position in the LOMBARTZYDE SECTOR. Preparations for the move were at once made.	R.D.
Battalion at COXYDE.	September 28, 1917.		The Battalion left COXYDE for the Line about 6 P.M. Major W.W. Morton being in command. The march forward was completed without incident and the Battalion again took	R.D.

WAR DIARY – SHEET 17.

of

INTELLIGENCE SUMMARY.

Army Form C. 2118.

Place	Date	Hour	Summary of Events and Information	Remarks and references to Appendices
	September 28 contd.		over the line which they had first been in. Sector A & B. Coys holding the forward system of defences with C. & D. Coys in support. A Defence Scheme was prepared and issued to Company Commanders, detailing action in case of attack. The enemy was pretty active during the night, sending over large numbers of shells, the GRAND REDAN and PETIT REDAN being particularly shelled.	R.1
	September 29, 1917.		Battalion in the Line. – Shelling continued heavily all day, our artillery replying at intervals. Casualties were comparatively slight, one man killed and 2 wounded.	R.2.
	September 30, 1917.		Battalion in the Line. – Work on the lines was carried on as usual. night and everything was done to strengthen and improve the defences. Shelling continued incessantly, NIEUPORT, the Canal, and the REDAN being heavily visited.	R.3.

END OF VOL. No. II

VOLUME 12

J. Ingles
Lt Colonel
Commanding 17th (S) Bn. H.L.I.

WAR DIARY SHEET
of
INTELLIGENCE SUMMARY.
(Erase heading not required)

Army Form C. 2118.

Place	Date	Hour	Summary of Events and Information	Remarks and references to Appendices
Battalion in the LINE.	October 1, 1917.	—	The enemy continued to shell the REDAN and the YSER Bridges with considerable intensity. In the early hours of the morning a carrying party of the 11th Border Regiment were caught by shell fire at a point near Battalion H.Q. A shell fell amongst the party, killing three and wounding four, the latter including two of our Battalion guides. A man belonging to B. Company who was in the vicinity was also wounded. Word was received at night that the Battalion would move into Reserve Positions on the following night, the relieving unit being the 11th Border Regt. Companies were to be distributed in reserve position in Dugouts at NEW PARADE, and the SARDINERIE (NIEUPORT) with platoons in the PRESQU'ILE Defences and in reserve trenches.	R.D.
Battalion in the LINE.	October 2, 1917.		Shelling was again heavy overnight. In the early morning the enemy raided one of our advanced posts (Solomon R.D.) and gained a temporary footing in it by means of a new device. A strong stream of water, apparently from a hose were suddenly turned upon our men from an adjacent enemy post. The men in our post were taken by surprise and blinded	R.D.

WAR DIARY or INTELLIGENCE SUMMARY

Army Form C. 2118.

Place	Date	Hour	Summary of Events and Information	Remarks and references to Appendices
	Oct 2, cont'd.		by the well. The post was then bombed, and the two listeners retired on the main post for support. There an immediate counter attack was organised by Sergt./Sgt. Major Millar. A. Coy. Under covering fire a party from the main post led by him advanced on the enemy and our post was re-established. A patrol then went out, but no trace of the enemy was found. L.A.M. Miller, for his prompt action, has since been awarded the Military Cross. The day was a little quieter, but there was the usual heavy shelling of NIEUPORT, the BRIDGES and the REDAN. Relief was carried out at night in accordance with the Brigade Order. One casualty was reported in A. Coy. when their relief was in progress, but the perilous crossing of the YSER was effected without loss.	
	October 3, 1917.		Battalion at NEW PARADE. Once established in Reserve positions no time was lost in seeing to the strength and efficiency of companies after the trying spell in the front line. During the early hours of the morning following relief there was some shelling of the new positions. The day was comparatively quiet. At night parties from C. & D. Companies left for work in the line.	
	October 4, 1917.		Battalion at NEW PARADE. Warning was received that Divisional Relief	

WAR DIARY SHEET 3.
or
INTELLIGENCE SUMMARY.

Army Form C. 2118.

Place	Date	Hour	Summary of Events and Information	Remarks and references to Appendices
Oct 4	Oct 4		would take place on the night 5/6th October, the seals being taken over by the 42nd Division. Raid advances pending the relieving Division carried for the purpose of making a return to the line an	
Oct 5	5.19.17.		Battalion at NEW PARADE.— Work in the front line aften carried out overnight. Brigade Operation Orders were received in the morning showing that the relief of the 91st Infantry Brigade would be effected by the 125th Infantry Brigade. The relief took place at night. The incoming unit - the 2nd Lancs,- sustained several casualties on taking over, being caught by enfilade fire from enemy machine guns whilst approaching NEW PARADE. No casualties were sustained by our Battalion. The road from NIEUPORT to COXYDE was negotiated in safety and the Battalion billeted in the latter place for the night.	
Oct 6	6.19.17.		Battalion at COXYDE.— The Battalion set out from COXYDE, early in the afternoon for ADINKERKE where the men were embarked on barges the journey was continued by canal to a point midway between ZUYDCOOTE and ROSSNDHEL and thence by road to UXEM	

WAR DIARY SHEET 4.
or
INTELLIGENCE SUMMARY.

Army Form C. 2118.

(Erase heading not required.)

Instructions regarding War Diaries and Intelligence Summaries are contained in F.S. Regs., Part II. and the Staff Manual respectively. Title pages will be prepared in manuscript.

Place	Date	Hour	Summary of Events and Information	Remarks and references to Appendices
	Oct. 6. contd.		Where billets were taken over in the village and neighbouring farms. Lieut. Colonel J. Inglis returned from leave and resumed command of the Battalion.	
	October 7, 1917.		Battalion at UXEM.- Church parades were held in the forenoon, the R.C. Services being in the Church, UXEM. the inclemency of the weather, however, prevailed the Presbyterian open-air service taking place. The weather continued stormy all day and for the most part Companies remained in billets cleaning up.	
	October 8, 1917.		Battalion at UXEM.- The day was passed quietly pending arrangements being made for the selection of a suitable Battalion training ground. Inspection of billets and ordinary routine was carried out, and specialists paraded for instruction under specialist officers.	
	October 9, 1917.		Battalion at UXEM.- Work on similar lines was carried out, the men being allowed to rest as much as possible. A pay-out was made during the afternoon. Arrangements were made for the Battalion football team to play a team from the P. Lockman A.S.C.	

Army Form C. 2118.

WAR DIARY SHEET 5.
or
INTELLIGENCE SUMMARY.
(Erase heading not required.)

Instructions regarding War Diaries and Intelligence Summaries are contained in F. S. Regs., Part II. and the Staff Manual respectively. Title pages will be prepared in manuscript.

Place	Date	Hour	Summary of Events and Information	Remarks and references to Appendices
October	10, 1917.		Battalion at LIXEM. — Specialist training continued, and clothing deficiencies were made good. The proposed football match was postponed, but purchases were made of various sporting requisites for the use of the men while out of the line. A circulating library was also started, under the charge of the Chaplain, with a number of books which had been forwarded to the Battalion from home. Orders were issued at night detailing training operations for the following day in the Wöelfer Training Area.	n.a.
October	11, 1917.		Battalion at LIXEM. — Companies marched to the training ground in the morning where operations were carried out in accordance with a pre-arranged training scheme. Rations were carried and the whole day was passed in training.	n.a.
October	12, 1917.		Battalion at LIXEM. — A change in the weather conditions interfered to some extent with the training programme, but drill and specialist instruction were carried out under Company arrangements. The third round of the Guard Mounting Competition which was inaugurated by the Commanding Officer when the Battalion was	n.a.

WAR DIARY
INTELLIGENCE SUMMARY.
(Erase heading not required.)

Army Form C. 2118.

WAR DIARY SHEET 6

Instructions regarding War Diaries and Intelligence Summaries are contained in F.S. Regs., Part II. and the Staff Manual respectively. Title pages will be prepared in manuscript.

Place	Date	Hour	Summary of Events and Information	Remarks and references to Appendices
October	12. 1917.		was at GHYVELDE in August, was carried through, "C" Company's Guard scoring highest marks on this occasion. In the evening the Divisional Machine Gun Officer delivered a lecture for Officers in the School-house, LIXEM.	
October	13. 1917.		Battalion at LIXEM.— Ordinary training routine continued, particular attention being paid to the training of specialists. The heavy rain in the afternoon interfered with arrangements for a football match to be played on the Battalion parade ground. The fourth round of the Guard Mounting Competition had also to be postponed on account of the weather.	
October	14. 1917.		Battalion at LIXEM.— Church parade for all denominations were the principal feature of the day's proceedings. R.C. again attended service in LIXEM Church. A football match between the Battalion team and a team from the H.S.C. was played in the afternoon, the Battalion eleven winning by 5 goals to 0.	
October	15. 1917.		Battalion at LIXEM.— Training was continued as before. Nothing of particular note occurred during the day. In the evening the	

Army Form-C. 2118.

WAR DIARY
or
INTELLIGENCE SUMMARY.
(Erase heading not required)

Instructions regarding War Diaries and Intelligence Summaries are contained in F. S. Regs., Part II. and the Staff Manual respectively. Title pages will be prepared in manuscript.

Place	Date	Hour	Summary of Events and Information	Remarks and references to Appendices
	Oct. 15 cont.		Commanding Officer lectured to Officers and Platoon commanders in the School-Salle LIXEM.	M7
	October 16, 1917.		Battalion at LIXEM. — There were no changes in the training programme, but bitter weather conditions precluded training to be fully taken advantage of. Observations were posted for one of Battalion helping tournament and on entertainment was arranged to play a team from the R.I.F.C. on the following day.	M7
	October 17, 1917.		Battalion at LIXEM. — Another quiet day followed. Training being carried on to the best advantage. The match between the R.I.F. team and our eleven resulted in a win for us by 3 goals to nil. An Operation Order was issued in this evening detailing manoeuvres to take place on the following day at FORT LES DUNES.	M7
	October 18, 1917.		Battalion at LIXEM. The practice attack formulated in the Operation Order was successfully carried out. The enemy (the 1114 Brigade Regiment) were assumed to be holding a position in the DUNES which the Battalion was to attack and capture. The attack was made on a two Company frontage "A" and "B" Companies forming the first and second waves. The first objectives were attacked and	M7

Army Form C. 2118.

WAR DIARY SHEET 8.
or
INTELLIGENCE SUMMARY.
(Erase heading not required.)

Place	Date	Hour	Summary of Events and Information	Remarks and references to Appendices
	Oct 18, cont'd		captured within scheduled time, A and B then consolidating whilst C and D. Companies, forming the third and fourth waves passed through and obtained the final objective. The advance was made under a barrage represented by flags progressing forward in 50 yards leaps and the men were practised in keeping well within the cover of the barrage while moving with it. After the demonstration the Battalion marched back to billets, and there was a pay-out in the evening.	
	October 19, 1917.		Battalion at UXEM. — A Battalion route march took place, the purpose being to inculcate discipline and men in the various points of march discipline. The route taken was from Billet, — LEFRINCKOUCKE — SALGHOECK — WAGCHENBRUGGHE — UXEM. En route the men were practised in taking off and putting on their equipment within specified time during halts. In the afternoon various heats of the Boxing Tournament were decided.	
	October 20, 1917.		Battalion at UXEM. — The Battalion marched to the Battalion Training Area for special Company instruction and training on lines detailed in a programme submitted to Company Commanders. After the men fell in in the afternoon the rest of the day was passed quietly.	

WAR DIARY SHEET 9.
INTELLIGENCE SUMMARY.

Army Form C. 2118.

Place	Date	Hour	Summary of Events and Information	Remarks and references to Appendices
October	21, 1917.		Battalion at LIXEM. — Church parade were held. R.C.'s attending Mass in LIXEM Church. In the afternoon friendlies were decided and football was played.	AP.
October	22, 1917.		Battalion at LIXEM. — Companies paraded in the forenoon for demonstrations as taught at the XVIII Corps School. Route marches followed, the route taken being similar to that of the 19th inst. Specialist training was also carried on. A lecture on the Bourbes was delivered in the School house in the evening by Major Summer, R.E. A warning order was received via Company Commanders in the evening intimating that the Battalion would move from the AREA on Wednesday 24th inst.	AP.
October	23, 1917.		Battalion at LIXEM.— The day was passed quietly ordinary routine being carried out. Operation Orders detailing the following day's march were issued to Company. In the evening the Musical Officers lectured in the School house.	AP.
October	24, 1917.		Battalion EN ROUTE. — The Battalion left LIXEM in the forenoon for the ERINGHEM Area in accordance with the forward move of the Brigade Group. The route followed from LIXEM was by road to HOYMILLE - SOEHX -	AP.

Place	Date	Hour	Summary of Events and Information	Remarks and references to Appendices
Oct 24 contd.			ZEGGERS-CAPPEL.- No further conditions rendered the march. The men were in fine fettle and maintained an unbroken formation throughout, eliciting the commendation of the Corps Commander who watched the march past. Further praise of the appearance and march discipline of the Battalion was given by a Brigadier Major of the 9th Division who passed the Battalion en route. Temporary billets were reached in the afternoon in the "D" Area, and the men rested during the evening in preparation for a continuation of the march on the following day, to the ROUBROUCK Area.	[n.]
October 25, 1917.			Battalion at Rest.- The march was continued in the forenoon to AREA "F" ROUBROUCK. full kit was carried, but despite the heavy march of the previous day the Battalion completed the journey without incident. On arrival in the new billets arrangements were at once made for carrying on with routine and orders were issued detailing the work for the following day.	[n.]

Army Form C. 2118.

WAR DIARY Sheet N°.
or
INTELLIGENCE SUMMARY.
(Erase heading not required.)

Instructions regarding War Diaries and Intelligence Summaries are contained in F. S. Regs., Part II. and the Staff Manual respectively. Title pages will be prepared in manuscript.

Place	Date	Hour	Summary of Events and Information	Remarks and references to Appendices
October	26, 1917.		Battalion at BROXEELE. — The first full day in the new area was spent in completing detail and arranging for the carrying on of the training programme. In place of parades Companies spent the forenoon in cleaning up. There was a pay-out in the afternoon, and the men were free from duty for the rest of the day.	n.a.
October	27, 1917.		Battalion at BROXEELE. — Training was recommenced. The weather being favourable for out-of-door operations. A practice attack scheme was arranged by the Commanding Officer, and this was carried out in the evening by Companies.	n.a.
Oct 28, 1917.			Battalion at BROXEELE. — Church Parades were held in the Village and at RUBROUCK and Companies bathed during the day.	n.a.
October	29, 1917.		Battalion at BROXEELE. — Ordinary routine was resumed and commencing with inspections in the morning. Training included Bayonet fighting, Platoon attacks on Strong Point musketry, &c. The mean being arranged as far as possible with a view to training the men for forthcoming operations. Specialist work was also carried on and Battalion Assembly Parties were formed for instruction in their particular duties during an advance in attack.	n.a.

WAR DIARY SHEET 12
INTELLIGENCE SUMMARY

Army Form C. 2118.

Place	Date	Hour	Summary of Events and Information	Remarks and references to Appendices
October	30, 1917		Battalion at BROXEELE. - The Battalion paraded in the morning for a Brigade Inspection by the Divisional Commander who witnessed addressing the men. Unfortunately rain commenced to fall heavily just before the time for inspection, and the weather showed no signs of clearing, Companies were returned to their billets before reaching the parade ground. In view of the men having received a wetting, out-door work was limited for the rest of the day, Companies being permitted to kit and prepare for a practice attack on a large scale which was arranged for the early hours of next morning.	
October	31, 1917		Battalion at BROXEELE. - The rain abated but left the ground in a muddy condition, rendering the operation of the morning more difficult to realize. The scheme drawn up for the practise assumed the enemy to be holding an organised system of shell holes and "pill-box" defences. The Brigade was to attack on a 1800 yards frontage with three Battalions, K.O.Y.L.I. (right) 16th H.L.I. (Centre) 17th H.L.I. (Left) the 11th Border Regiment were in reserve as Counter counter-attack troops. The Battalions attack frontage was 700 yards. (The ground for commencement.)	

Army Form C. 2118.

WAR DIARY SHEET 13
or
INTELLIGENCE-SUMMARY.
(Erase heading not required.)

Instructions regarding War Diaries and Intelligence Summaries are contained in F. S. Regs., Part II. and the Staff Manual respectively. Title pages will be prepared in manuscript.

Place	Date	Hour	Summary of Events and Information	Remarks and references to Appendices
	Oct. 21 cont.		Having been previously told off. Companies advanced in "wave-formation" each having its special platoon objective. A and B. Companies composed the first attacking wave. C. & D. Companies forming in artillery formation in rear of A and B. respectively. The scheme worked out successfully, platoons advancing towards their objectives without confusion and under close cover of a creeping barrage. "Pill-boxes" and "strong-points" were attacked with enthusiasm. The Battalion returned to billets in the morning and the rest of the day was passed quietly.	m57

END OF VOLUME 12.

R. MacTaggart
Lieut.
2/Kent.

Intelligence Officer 1/4 R.W.K.

SECRET

17 HLI
Vol 25

WAR DIARY

From Nov 1, 1917
Till
Nov. 30, 1917.

VOL. No 13.

J Inglis. Rect Co Comd
Commanding 17th (S) Bn. H.L.I.

WAR DIARY
INTELLIGENCE SUMMARY

Army Form C. 2118.

Place	Date	Hour	Summary of Events and Information	Remarks and references to Appendices
	November 1, 1917.		**Battalion at BROXEELE.** — During the absence of the Commanding Officer — Lieut. Col. J. Inglis, and the Adjutant - Captain L.G. Gunner - who were making a tour of inspection of the line on the YPRES front, Captain T.D. Russell M.C. "D" Company assumed command of the Battalion. The routine for the day included company inspections, musketry, and further practice in attacking "strong points". Specialists paraded under officer instructors for training. Roman Catholics paraded under the Orderly Officer, in the forenoon, and marched to BROXEELE Church where Confessions were heard. The Divisional Commander's congratulations to 2nd Lt. M. Angus Miller, (A Company) on his being awarded the Military Cross in recognition of his promptness and courageous conduct during an enemy raid on one of our advanced posts on the night of October 1/2nd., were noted in Battalion Orders along with those of the Commanding Officer.	
	November 2, 1917.		**Battalion at BROXEELE.** — Routine proceeded on ordinary lines, Although the work for the day was devoted to some extent to renewed and setting drill. Official intimation was received that the Battalion would not probably go into the line for about three weeks. A training programme for the following week was drawn up, and preparations were made for taking part, the following evening in a practice attack scheme arranged by the 97th Infantry Brigade.	

Army Form C. 2118.

WAR DIARY — Sheet 2.
or
INTELLIGENCE SUMMARY.

Instructions regarding War Diaries and Intelligence Summaries are contained in F.S. Regs., Part II. and the Staff Manual respectively. Title pages will be prepared in manuscript.

Place	Date	Hour	Summary of Events and Information	Remarks and references to Appendices
	November 3, 1917.		Battalion at BROXEELE. — The practice scheme was carried out at night. The intention of the Scheme was to perfect the Brigade in moving into a line which was assumed to have been taken and consolidated 48 hours previously by the 11th Border Regt. On Y-Z night the remainder of the Brigade were to move to Assembly positions, the Border Regt. being relieved and moving to the rear as counter-attack troops for the attack at dawn. The object of obtaining experience in forming up in assembly positions and moving off captured ground in the dark, was fulfilled successfully.	AHM
	November 4, 1917.		Battalion at BROXEELE. — Church services were held. Communion in BROXEELE School, and mass in the Church. There was also a memorial service to the late Rev. Captain Langdon, C.F. (11th Border Regt.), who was killed during the previous week, by an enemy bomb, whilst on a tour of the YPRES front. D. Company worked on the Range all day, and in the afternoon the Battalion team played a team of the 15th. H.L.I. at football, winning by 2 goals to 1.	AHM
	November 5, 1917.		Battalion at BROXEELE. — Ordinary routine was carried on, training being on the lines laid down in the Programme. B. Company were on the Range.	AHM
	November 6, 1917.		Battalion at BROXEELE. — Training continued on lines similar to those of the preceding days. Bombers, signallers, Lewis gunners and Assembly Parties each parading under their respective officers for instruction.	AHM

Army Form C. 2118.

WAR DIARY - SHEET 3.
INTELLIGENCE SUMMARY.

Place	Date	Hour	Summary of Events and Information	Remarks and references to Appendices
	Nov. 7, 1917.		Battalion at BROXEELE. - The training programme was suspended for the day, the Battalion, instead, being deputed to assist in a Brigade manoeuvre. Unfortunately, adverse weather interfered with the project and the Battalion had to return to billets. The rest of the day was spent in cleaning up in preparation for the Corps Commander's inspection on the following day. Company Commanders were instructed to see that the Divisional Routine Order regarding destruction of property or discourtesy to the civilian population were read to the men on Parade in order that the consequences of such action might be impressed upon them. In the afternoon the Battalion Football team met the team of the 2nd K.O.Y.L.I. A splendid game resulted, but our men were in their best form, and defeated the Royalies by 5 goals to 1, thus placing the Batt. in the final of the Brigade tournament.	
	November 8, 1917.		Battalion at BROXEELE. - The Battalion paraded in the morning over 700 strong and marched to the Parade Ground RUBROUCH for inspection by the Corps Commander. Everything had been done to ensure that the Battalion turned out scrupulously clean in every detail, and in the bright weather which favoured the proceedings, the men bearing very efficient. The Corps Commander was unable to be present, but in his absence the Brigade was inspected by Major-General C.D. SHUTE, C.B., C.M.G., Commanding 32nd. Division.	

WAR DIARY SHEET - 4.
INTELLIGENCE SUMMARY.

Army Form C. 2118.

Instructions regarding War Diaries and Intelligence Summaries are contained in F. S. Regs., Part II. and the Staff Manual respectively. Title pages will be prepared in manuscript.

(Erase heading not required).

Place	Date	Hour	Summary of Events and Information	Remarks and references to Appendices
	November 9, 1917		**Battalion at BROXEELE.** — Information was received that the Battalion would leave BROXEELE on the following day and proceed to the FORWARD AREA. Preparations were made for the move and orders issued detailing the order of march, etc.	AH
	November 10, 1917		**Battalion at BROXEELE.** — The Battalion left BROXEELE in the morning and marched via RUBROUCK - ARNEKE - LEDRINGHEM and WORMHOUDT, halting for the night in huts outside WORMHOUDT. The roads and the nature of the weather made marching very arduous, but despite these adverse circumstances the Battalion completed the first part of the forward move in good time. A feature of the march was the meeting en route with the 2nd. Y.L.I. who were also billetted outside of WORMHOUDT. There were many recognitions and much fraternisation between original members of the 17th still with the Battalion and those now with the 2nd.	AH
	November 11, 1917		**Battalion En Route.** — The move was continued the following morning via HERZEELE - HOUTKERQUE - WATOU to ROAD CAMP in the ST. JAN TER BIEZEN Area where the men were accommodated in NISSEN HUTS and in tents. On arrival the men were rested after their long and trying march.	AH
	November 12, 1917		**Battalion at ROAD CAMP.** — The first day in the new Quarters began quietly. Musketry training was suspended for the day to allow of a general cleaning up. Companies carried out feet inspection and anti-	AH

WAR DIARY - SHEET 5.
INTELLIGENCE SUMMARY.

Place	Date	Hour	Summary of Events and Information	Remarks and references to Appendices
Nov. 12, 1917			Trench Foot treatment under the supervision of officers.	
	November 13, 1917.		Battalion at ROAD CAMP. — The men being refreshed and fit again training was resumed. The weather had again become dry and more freedom of movement was thus permitted over the much-covered ground. Trench foot treatment was continued and in the forenoon and afternoon the Battalion had the use of vapour baths situated in the Camp. Captain R. Dow, the Medical Officer left the Battalion having been posted to the 91st Division and his place was taken by Captain Pugh of the United States Army. In the evening the massed pipe bands of the 16th and 17th H.L.I. played on the Camp Parade ground. All day and night the roll of artillery fire was audible from the front, then at times attaining great intensity.	
	November 14, 1917.		Battalion at ROAD CAMP. — Training proceeded in customary line, Signallers and messengers of the Battalion, along with those of the BRIGADE and the 11th BORDER REGT carried out a practice alarm in forward communication in battle. The afternoon was mainly devoted to sport, the Battalion team and that of the 16th H.L.I. meeting in the final of the Brigade tournament. Fine weather favoured the occasion and a large crowd of spectators from both Battalions enjoyed an exciting game. Our men were undefeated, the better team faster, and more	

Army Form C. 2118.

WAR DIARY — SHEET 6.
— or —
INTELLIGENCE SUMMARY.
(Erase heading not required.)

Instructions regarding War Diaries and Intelligence Summaries are contained in F. S. Regs., Part II. and the Staff Manual respectively. Title pages will be prepared in manuscript.

Place	Date	Hour	Summary of Events and Information	Remarks and references to Appendices
	Nov. 14 cont'd		co-ordinate, the began well and maintained their supremacy throughout winning the final by 5 goals to nil.	
	November 15, 1917.		Battalion at ROAD CAMP. — The training programme was followed in detail time being devoted to Gas Helmet drill, platoon attacks on strong-point, and forming-up practice. In the afternoon a team of the Battalion Officers met an officers' team of the 16th H.L.I., and maintained the Battalion's supremacy in football by defeating the 16th by 4 goals to nil.	A.M.M.
	November 16, 1917.		Battalion at ROAD CAMP. — The Divisional Commander paid a visit of inspection to the Camp during the forenoon, making a tour of the lines of both the 16th H.L.I. and our own. Training proceeded on the usual lines.	A.M.M.
	November 17, 1917.		Battalion at ROAD CAMP. — The greater part of the day was spent in a thorough cleaning-out and improving of the Camp. Huts were vacated by Companies and cleaned; blankets and clothing were also submitted to a cleansing process. An improvement was also effected in the draining of the Camp which was in a very muddy condition. Trenches were dug alongside the huts, and ductwork to carry off the accumulated water, and huts were afterwards more effectively sandbagged as a	A.M.M.

(A7032) Wt. W12839/M.2793. 75,000. 4/17. D. D. & L., Ltd. Forms/C.2118/14.

WAR DIARY SHEET 7.

INTELLIGENCE SUMMARY.

Army Form C. 2118.

Place	Date	Hour	Summary of Events and Information	Remarks and references to Appendices
	Nov.17. contd		protection against enemy bombs. The general scheme of overhauling occupied the whole day but the improvement made in the Camp was conspicuous. In the evening, a string Band composed of members of the Battalion gave their inaugural performance in a tent outside Headquarters Mess.	MHJ
	Nov. 18, 1917.		Battalion at ROAD CAMP. — The day being Sunday was spent quietly in the R.C. Services were held in St Jan-TER-BIEZEN Church. The Y.M.C.A. hut opposite the camp Battalion added to its sporting laurels by defeating the 32nd Divisional Supply Column in the semi-final of the Divisional Football Tournament. The match attracted a great crowd and credit themselves enthusiasm. It was fast and exciting throughout, the Battalion team having to come then went to bear in winning, which they did brilliantly up to half-time there was no scoring. Extra time was played, and the Supply Column scored shortly afterwards. The 17th equalized from a penalty and, a few minutes later, added another goal which decided the match.	MHJ
	November 19, 1917.		Battalion at ROAD CAMP. — Training was carried on as usual during this day. In the afternoon Battalion Officers and Warrant Officers & Sergeants met in a friendly match. The Officers winning by 3 goals to nil	MHJ

WAR DIARY
or
INTELLIGENCE SUMMARY

Army Form C. 2118.

Place	Date	Hour	Summary of Events and Information	Remarks and references to Appendices
	November 20, 1917.		**Battalion at ROAD CAMP.** - Sport was again the principal feature of the day, the afternoon being devoted to it also. The training and routine of the former was gone through. The occasion was the final of The Battalion football tournament in which the Battalion team played the 2nd Royal Innskilling Fusiliers. The match was decided in fine weather before a huge concourse of ototic spectators, and it was favoured by the presence of the Divisional Commander. The game proved a harand fought one, the "Skins" Eleven proving themselves worthy opponents. The first half saw no scoring but in the second half the Battalion team broke through and scored twice, thus winning the Championship, as they had done in the previous year against the same opponents. In the evening a warning Order was received that the 97th Infantry Brigade would move forward in the 22nd inst, of the Ypres front and prepare to relieve the 2nd Infantry Bde. (1st Division), in the line on the night 23/24th November. Officers were detailed to proceed to the line on a Recconnaissance the following morning.	
	November 21, 1917.		**Battalion at Road Camp.** - C.D. SHUTE, C.B., C.M.G., Major Gen. in the forenoon the Divisional Commander, Major Gen. was on the football ground to the rear of the Camp. He reviewed the men of the Brigade, Battalion being formed up in line of the storm drills, that now lay before them and expressed the hope	

WAR DIARY SHEET 9.
or
INTELLIGENCE SUMMARY.

Army Form C. 2118.

Place	Date	Hour	Summary of Events and Information	Remarks and references to Appendices
	November 21, contd.		that they wished maintain the honourable traditions associated with the name of the 97th Infantry Brigade.	
	November 22, 1917.		Battalion at ROAD CAMP. — The Battalion left the Camp for POPERINGHE where they entrained to continue their journey up-line. On arrival at ST. JEAN Station, the BRIGADE detrained and marched to IRISH CAMP where huts and 5 tents were taken over.	XXX
	November 28, 1917.		Battalion at IRISH CAMP. — The day was occupied with a general supervision of details and preparations for proceeding to the front line system in the evening. A start was made for the line about 8 P.M. the route taken by the Battalion being for the greater part over the duck-walks MOUSE TRAP TRACK which caused great delay in the recent Brig. Front at PASSCHENDAELE. Relief was not completed without casualties, but these were comparatively few considering the dangerous nature of the going which was entirely in the open. Our shell pitted ground. Our casualties for the night were 2 OR killed and 6 O.R. wounded. The Battalion relieved by the 17th was the 1st NORTHAMPTONSHIRE Batt. All the preliminary "strafing" which resulted in the casualties was comparatively quiet. The front line disposition were — A Company with two platoons of B. Company on the Right, D. Company on the left	XXX

WAR DIARY SHEET 10
INTELLIGENCE SUMMARY.
(Erase heading not required.)

Army Form C. 2118.

Place	Date	Hour	Summary of Events and Information	Remarks and references to Appendices
	Nov. 23, contd.		"C" Company in support, and the remaining platoon of "B" in Reserve. Battalion Headquarters and the first Aid Post were established at IRON PRINZ FARM, a captured German PILLBOX. During the night the Battalion captured 1st prisoner in the area - a corporal of the 315th. REGIMENT. According to prisoners statements he had been out on patrol when he lost one of his boots in the mud, and in trying to find it he strayed into our lines and was taken prisoner.	[signature]
	November 24, 1917.		Battalion in the LINE. - As one on the line was vigourously shelled on the system of shell-hole defenses being converted into trenches, organised as far as the nature of the ground would permit. Shell fire on the line was not exceptionally active, but the areas immediately behind and the duck were tracks received considerable attention. Consolidation and reconnaissances of the RIDGE in view of the forthcoming offensive were carried on. Patrols were also actively engaged during the day and nighttime, reconnoitring possible PILL BOX Strongholds in front of our line, but none of the enemy were encountered. During the night, a second prisoner, who had been taken by the RIGHT BATTN. (the 2nd. 11.0.Y.L.I.) was brought to Battalion HEADQUARTERS for preliminary interrogation. Shelling continued throughout the day and night	[signature]

WAR DIARY SHEET II
INTELLIGENCE SUMMARY

Army Form C. 2118.

Place	Date	Hour	Summary of Events and Information	Remarks and references to Appendices
Nor. 24 contd			increasing in intensity at times, but casualties were again comparatively light.	DAM
	November 25, 1917.		Battalion in the Line. – The final day of the Battalion's initial tour in the PASSCHEN- DAELE Line was marked for an increase in the number of casualties. Throughout the day there was little in the nature of heavy shelling, but towards night, no relief was in progress heavy artillery fire developed on our light, sweeping along the line and visiting the duckwalk tracks severely. Casualties in Left the Battalion Receiving the Fire and Also Effecting the Relief were pretty heavy and Battalion Headquarters an advanced aid post, comes scarcely accommodating all the wounded. Losses were especially drastic by the Medical Officers and his staff. Among our wounded were 2nd Lieut. R. M^c FADZEAN, the Battalion Intelligence Officer, who received a bullet wound in the left arm whilst engaged in taping off ground. The artillery duel continued for some time on both sides, S.O.S. signals going up from our lines, but after a while it died down, and relief was then completed. The 11th BORDER REGIMENT taking over our line. The total casualties for the tour were 97 including killed, wounded and 2 missing.	DAM
	November 26, 1917.		Battalion at DAMBRE CAMP. – After relief the Battalion proceeded to HILLTOP FARM	DAM

WAR DIARY. SHEET 12.
INTELLIGENCE SUMMARY.

Army Form C. 2118.

Place	Date	Hour	Summary of Events and Information	Remarks and references to Appendices
	November 26 contd.		There the night was spent, and in the afternoon following the men entrained and marched part of the way, journey to DAMBRE CAMP in the VLAMERTINGHE Area. The men were rested and arrangements made for re-organisation and cleaning up on the following day.	MMM
	November 27, 1917		Battalion at DAMBRE CAMP. - The men the did themselves the men had a period in comparative quiet to enable fire in the line caused the PASSCHENDAELE shell holes. Artillery to great intensity at times. Our artillery active all day the firing developing enemy intermittently shelled in the direction of VLAMERTINGHE with H.E. shells. We replied with a heavy barrage fire.	MMM
	November 28, 1917		Battalion at DAMBRE CAMP. - Training was again resumed we being made of firing ranges in the camp. The day was uneventful except for the occasional overhead return of enemy shells which were dropped all round the area. Brigade Orders were received for the Offensive during the course of the next few days and arrangements were immediately made to have these become operative.	MMM
	November 29, 1917		Battalion at DAMBRE CAMP. - Further arrangements was made in connection with the forthcoming Offensive the Commanding Officer meeting Company Commanders in conference and arranging details with them Officers and N.C.O's visited Divisional Headquarters for inspection of a relief map	MMM

Army Form C. 2118.

WAR DIARY SHEET 13
INTELLIGENCE SUMMARY.

Place	Date	Hour	Summary of Events and Information	Remarks and references to Appendices
? Potenche	29omb.		of the area on the Ridge had by us, and the ground to be taken.	
	November 30, 1919.		Battalion at DAMBRE CAMP. In the forenoon the Commanding Officer visited 2 Companies in the Y.M.C.A. tent, and shortly afterwards the Battalion left DAMBRE CAMP to entrain for HILLTOP FARM in the forward area. Shelling of the area vacated was rather active all day, but no shells fell within 1 camp area.	[initials]

[signature] Lieut. Colonel
Commanding 17th (S.) Bn. H.L.I.

17 HL 197/32
VA 26

3rd 15th Batalion H.L.I.

WAR DIARY

FROM. DECEMBER 1, 1917
TO " 31, 1917.

VOL. II.

A.B. Martin
MAJOR
COMMANDING 1/15 Batt. H.L.I.

WAR DIARY SHEET 1.
or
INTELLIGENCE SUMMARY.

Army Form C. 2118.

Place	Date	Hour	Summary of Events and Information	Remarks and references to Appendices
December 12.19.17			Battalion in the Line. – The Battalion moved into the Line in the evening, in conjunction with the other Battalions of the Brigade – the 2nd. K.O.Y.L.I., the 16th A.L.I., the 11th Border Regt, and the 15th Lancs. Fusiliers (attached). The 15th Northumberland Fusiliers (96th Inf. Bde.), were attached to the 97th Inf. Bde. as counter attacking troops, to be used in the event of a strong hostile counter attack on the Brigade front. The Frontage taken over by the Brigade was one of 1850 yards, running approximately along Passchendaele Ridge from Tournant Farm, on the right, to Teall Cott on the right. The disposition of Battalions was as follows:– No.5 Battalion – the 15th Lancs. Fusiliers; No.4. Battalion – the 17th. H.L.I., No.3. Battalion – the 11th Border Regt, No.2. Battalion 16th. H.L.I, No.1. Battalion – 2nd. K.O.Y.L.I. The intention was to advance on this front at zero hour and drive the enemy from positions occupied by him on the Ridge. There was an objective to be taken – a Green Line, running approximately from Veal Cottages on our Battalion front, to a point just in rear of No. 3. Company No. 2. Battalion; and a Red Line running approximately from Tournant Farm on the Corps	99/v

WAR DIARY Sheet 2.
INTELLIGENCE SUMMARY.

Army Form C. 2118.

Place	Date	Hour	Summary of Events and Information	Remarks and references to Appendices
Beaumetz	1/2nd Oct.		BOUNDARY at a point opposite No.1. Company. No.1. Battalion. The 17th A.I.F. were responsible for the capture of the first objective from a point V.23.d.06.32. (Right of MALLET COPSE), to V.23.c.19.09.(-in front of) and to left of VERT COTTAGES), and facing in VAT COTTAGES. The second objective or RED LINE was from V.23.c.04.91 to V.23.c.13.42. The Battalion assembled on a frontage of 1100 yards from V.29.b.10.4 to V.29.a.30.45. the frontage on the first objective to be one of 500 yards. At ZERO HOUR – 1.55 a.m., the Battalion moved forward to the attack on a two Company frontage with 'C' and 'D' Companies in Rear of 'A' and 'B' Companies respectively. The enemy of artillery fire until ZERO plus 3 minute was, therefore, an unaware of the attack were to be surprised. The Companies deployed from their two "Platoon frontage" in SNAKE formation – this having been adopted owing to the rolling formation of the ground – and advanced in four waves, the distance between waves being 30 yards and between Companies, 40 yards. A. and B. Companies were detailed to advance as far as the "GREEN LINE" capturing and mopping up all occupied points on the way, including	

WAR DIARY SHEET 3.
INTELLIGENCE SUMMARY.

Place	Date	Hour	Summary of Events and Information	Remarks and references to Appendices
	December 2 contd.		The PILLBOXES known as VET and VEAL COTTAGES, 16 and 18 bompanies were to "Loop-frog" to the GREEN LINE and push forward to the RED LINE where consolidation was to take place and preparation made against a counter attack by the enemy. The initial stages of the attack, assembling etc, were successfully carried through, but the enemy - as was afterwards learned - had been apprised of our intentions and had made strong preparations against them. He opened heavy machine gun fire upon the advancing companies, inflicting heavy casualties which, in the dark, and over the difficult ground, had the effect of splitting up the sections and creating some confusion. Our men gallantly pressed forward against this odds, however, and succeeded in reaching their first objective. The enemy machine gun fire and rifle fire became so intense that advanced positions could not be rendered untenable. Our men though forced to fall back, established themselves in shell hole positions, and attempt was made to consolidate. The Barrage on our right had fallen across, passing all its objective. Our artillery and machine gun barrage, though intense, had failed, owing to the enemy's knowledge of the attack, to effect its purpose. His	

WAR DIARY SHEET 4.
or
INTELLIGENCE SUMMARY.

Army Form C. 2118.

Place	Date	Hour	Summary of Events and Information	Remarks and references to Appendices
Dec 1/2 contd			strong points were found to be heavily garrisoned and wired, and it was also found to be established in a strong line of trench also effectively wired. The Battalion hung on all night in its isolated position and orders were received that the attack would be resumed in the morning, but this order was afterwards cancelled. From dawn onwards artillery fire observed somewhat, but the enemy machine gunners and snipers kept up a harassing fire from their well established posts against our men in their exposed and isolated positions. It was obvious that a hostile counter attack might be expected and this took place about 4 P.M. on the afternoon of the 2nd. Preceded by an intense artillery barrage. It was exactly equally accurate and very heavy, but owing to difficulty of communication and the heavy casualties amongst Officers and N.C.O's and [crossed out] for the [crossed out] for the most part our original position. It appears that following our barrage the enemy attacked with one battalion which considerably cut up by our counter-fire came within a certain distance of our positions and then broke and	BM.

WAR DIARY SHEET 5.
INTELLIGENCE SUMMARY.

Army Form C. 2118.

Place	Date	Hour	Summary of Events and Information	Remarks and references to Appendices
Bec 1/2 ended			retired. The attack, and counter attack, although our efforts a failure, has on account of unexpected difficulties, only succeeded.	AAH.
Beaumont	Dec 2, 1917		Battalion in the line. — Through the withdrawal to our old line has been pretty general, some of our posts are being on in advance positions, and fires almost impossible at present to obtain an accurate estimate of casualties. There were roughly speaking at over 200, including killed, wounded and missing. Many wounded were lying out, and our Battalion stretcher bearers showed great devotion to duty in bringing the wounded in under fire. The work was of a most extremely dangerous nature during the day, a lull occurred when it was possible to carry on this labour under less trying conditions. From this point onwards the enemy showed great respect for the Red Cross flag, and only one instance of sniping being observed when our stretcher bearers were killed whilst tending our own shell-torn ⸺ losses were killed whilst tending our wounded men. Enemy stretcher-bearers were also at work, and in some instance they reciprocated our attentions to their wounded by drawing and carrying our casualties.	AAH.

Army Form C. 2118.

WAR DIARY SHEET 6.
INTELLIGENCE SUMMARY.

Place	Date	Hour	Summary of Events and Information	Remarks and references to Appendices
Page 3	Cont'd		In this way all the wounded were got in before the Barrage was relieved. That is Cpt. Com. Patterson Barrage was successfully was by the 5/10 & Royal Scots. Relief was successfully completed and the Battalion reached HILLTOP FARM in the early morning. The men rested until the afternoon when they entrained at ST JEAN Station for HOSPITAL CAMP in the VLAMERTINGHE area. The rest of the day was passed quietly, the men being allowed to clean up and attain a good rest in Andenne Camp in the P.m. The casualties for the tour were :- KILLED 41, WOUNDED 130, MISSING 13. Details as follows:-	

OFFICERS

KILLED	WOUNDED	MISSING
2nd Lt. J. OSBORNE	CAPT. S.O. WESTWATER	NIL
" R.N. CUNNINGHAM	2nd Lt. G.T. M°INTOSH	
" R.H. REID	" R.D.W. NICHOLSON	
" M. CAMERON	" R. SMITH	
" J. MILLER	" G. FORSYTH	
" W. MORLAND	(Lt. T.M.B.)	
(Lt. T.M.B.)		
2nd Lt. R.D. BROWN		
(died of wounds)		

OTHER RANKS.

KILLED - 41
WOUNDED - 130
MISSING - 13.

WAR DIARY SHEET 7.
INTELLIGENCE SUMMARY.

Army Form C. 2118.

(Erase heading not required.)

Instructions regarding War Diaries and Intelligence Summaries are contained in F. S. Regs., Part II. and the Staff Manual respectively. Title pages will be prepared in manuscript.

Place	Date	Hour	Summary of Events and Information	Remarks and references to Appendices
	Dec. 3, 1917		The previous town by the Brigade during the fighting numbered 40, of which 3 were captured by the Battalion. For MAP REFERENCES see Sheet 10,000 SPRIET.	SSM
	December 4, 1917		Battalion at HOSPITAL CAMP. – Parades were commenced to have the Battalion reorganised as far as possible in its depleted condition. Deficiencies made good and training resumed. Particular importance was attached to the treatment of prostration men fast in a fermentative against trench feet or frostbite, nothing as all Companies becoming a part of the daily routine.	SSM
	December 5, 1917		Battalion at HOSPITAL CAMP. – Training was resumed on a modified scale, the Battalion having formed for the time being on a Two Company basis until such time as it was again brought up to strength.	SSM
	December 6, 1917		Battalion at HOSPITAL CAMP. – In addition to daily training parties were provided for work under the supervision of the Commanding.	SSM

WAR DIARY SHEET 8.
INTELLIGENCE SUMMARY.

Army Form C. 2118.

Place	Date	Hour	Summary of Events and Information	Remarks and references to Appendices
Dec. 6 1917.			Commanded in maintaining the high standard of cleanliness of the camp. Companies paraded for bath at SIEGE CAMP where clean change of underclothing was also supplied.	
December 7, 1917.			Battalion at HOSPITAL CAMP. — Work parties averaging 150 strong were detailed for work in the lines under the R.E. on the laying of timber roads and Karak. Arrangements made for the inspection by the CORPS COMMANDER were cancelled, and instead, the Battalion paraded to hear an address from the Brigadier A.C. BLACKLOCK, D.S.O., Commanding 99th INFANTRY BRIGADE. This took place on the camp football ground. The Brigadier addressed the men not to be disheartened at the result of the attack, assuring them that they had done their utmost against great odds and pointing out that they would profit by what they had learned on their excursion when they again went into the line.	AGM
December 8, 1917.			Battalion at HOSPITAL CAMP. — Nothing of unusual interest occurred during the day. Work parties were again detailed for the line and ordinary routine was observed. In the afternoon the Battalion team, somewhat depleted by it former strength, — met the team of the 18th H.L.I. and suffered defeat on a	AGM

WAR DIARY
or
INTELLIGENCE SUMMARY.

Army Form C. 2118.

Place	Date	Hour	Summary of Events and Information	Remarks and references to Appendices
Dec. 8	cont'd		Difficult ground, after a hard hike. Score - 18 k. h goals; 174. 2. Intimation was received that the Battalion would again mount guard on the 10th inst.	99 r
	December 9, 1917.		Battalion at HOSPITAL CAMP. — Preparations were made for the service and divine services were held in one of the huts. The day otherwise was uneventful.	99 r
	December 10, 1917.		Battalion at HILLTOP FARM. — The Battalion vacated HOSPITAL CAMP shortly after noon and proceeded by route march to HILLTOP FARM, N.E. of YPRES where the men were accommodated in huts. Working parties for the Line were detailed on arrival and the remainder of the new quarters in the afternoon. The hostile gunfire was within range of the Camp which caused five men & another the eruption of one shell wounded five men & another unit, the Camp was free from enemy attention during the day.	99 r
	December 11, 1917.		Battalion at HILLTOP FARM. — The comparative immunity of the Camp from shell fire was disturbed on the evening of the 11th when enemy shells fell amongst the huts, at intervals of about a quarter of an hour. Though the shelling was rather heavy and continuous casualties were not exceptional. One shell dropped through the corrugated	99 r

Army Form C. 2118.

WAR DIARY SHEET 10.

INTELLIGENCE SUMMARY.

Instructions regarding War Diaries and Intelligence Summaries are contained in F. S. Regs., Part II. and the Staff Manual respectively. Title pages will be prepared in manuscript.

(Erase heading not required.)

Place	Date	Hour	Summary of Events and Information	Remarks and references to Appendices
(cont.)			roof of a hut occupied by No. 16 Platoon of D. Company, where 25 men were at the time, and burst, blowing out the greater part of the hut. Most of the men in the hut were thrown about, but the explosion and all were bruised and shaken, but, with this exception of one man who was found later in a shell hole no one was wounded.	
	December 12, 1917.		Battalion at HILLTOP FARM. — The day was uneventful as far as shelling of the camp was concerned but there was considerable aerial activity. In the afternoon two enemy aviators flew over the camp, at a low altitude. They were heavily shelled by Anti-Aircraft batteries and met with machine gun fire, and several of our planes at rest in pursuit. The enemy planes turned and made off in the direction of their own lines again, but before we proceeded far, when one of them was brought down in flames. The other machine was also hit, but the pilot managed to maintain control until he landed within our lines. He attempted to escape but was found upon and wounded and was then taken prisoner.	29th
	December 13, 1917.		Battalion at HILLTOP FARM. — Work on the GENOA TRACK was continued by parties supplied from the Battalion. The day was uneventful. Drill	

Army Form C. 2118.

WAR DIARY SHEET 11.
INTELLIGENCE SUMMARY.

Place	Date	Hour	Summary of Events and Information	Remarks and references to Appendices
	Dec. 13 contd.		weather hindering aerial observation. Artillery action was persistent on both sides and at nightfall it developed somewhat on both sides. The enemy searching our batteries with high explosive. Several shells landed close to the Camp but no damage was caused to any of the huts.	189m
	December 14th 1917.		Battalion at HILLTOP FARM. - Work continued within and without the line. The day was again dull and artillery consequently slack, with the approach of night however it again developed, the enemy being active with high velocity shells, the whole passed without any casualties occurring. Md Lieut. A. Barrell, the well known Scottish athlete visited the Battalion on a commission from the Corporation of Glasgow, to present drawings of the Glasgow Battalion and the scenes in which they were operating. Companies were informed that the Battalion would go into the line in the Right Sub-Sector on the night 17/18th. December. The new Regimental-Sergeant-Major R.S.M. BURNS, who assumed the night previous to charge of a small draft of reinforcements including C.Q.M.S. TURNER and DAY, - took over his duties from Acting R.S.M. HIRST.	18h
	December 15 1917		Battalion at HILLTOP FARM. - The day passed uneventfully. During the forenoon the Commanding Officer held a muster parade of the	

WAR DIARY SHEET 12.
or
INTELLIGENCE SUMMARY.

(Erase heading not required)

Army Form C. 2118.

Instructions regarding War Diaries and Intelligence Summaries are contained in F. S. Regs., Part II. and the Staff Manual respectively. Title pages will be prepared in manuscript.

Place	Date	Hour	Summary of Events and Information	Remarks and references to Appendices
	Dec. 15 cont'd		Battalion in Camp prior to their again going into the Line.	
	December 16, 1917		Battalion at HILLTOP FARM. – Usual parades were held in the forenoon and the remainder of the day was passed in preparing for going into the line. Towards evening the enemy shelled rather heavily around the area of the Camp, but there were no casualties.	1830hr
	December 17, 1917		Battalion at HILLTOP FARM. – The Battalion paraded about 3 P.M. and left Camp for the Line, taking over the same ground previously held. The going in was achieved without accident. Battalion Headquarters were established at POINT 83, the Unit relieved being the 15th LANCS. FUSILIERS. The night passed comparatively quiet in the RIGHT SECTOR only one slight casualty being reported.	8.9hr
	December 18, 1917		Battalion in the LINE. – Conditions on the front were very severe as regards weather, heavy frost and fog prevailing. The muddy, boggy and shell pitted ground became frozen and this with the preceding mist, enabled patrolling and reconnoitring to be actively carried out. Shelling was intermittent day and night but no further casualties were reported.	8.9hr
	December 19, 1917		Battalion in the LINE. – The weather remained severe but enemy activities were not increased. Patrolling and general improvements of the Line were carried out. At night one of our patrols pushed	

WAR DIARY SHEET 13.

or

INTELLIGENCE SUMMARY.

(Erase heading not required.)

Army Form C. 2118.

Place	Date	Hour	Summary of Events and Information	Remarks and references to Appendices
Dec 19	contd.		out, and occupied our enemy front. One prisoner was taken during the morning. A party of the enemy were observed through the (fog) and were dispersed by machine gun fire. The prisoner stumbling into our lines and talking to B. Company.	AAA
	December 20, 1917		Battalion in the Line. — The final day in the line was passed in comparative quiet, with shelling in the 11th BORDER REGIMENT . At night the Battalion were relieved by the 1/7th OFFORD Coys. and proceeded down line to WURST FARM in Brigade Support. One casualty occurred on relief, a sergeant of D. Company being wounded. O'Kennei. Relief was completed without incident.	AAA
	December 21, 1917		Battalion at WURST FARM. — During the day at WURST FARM the Battalion continued to carry out works on the line, information and strengthening of defences being regularly pushed forward. Large quantities of salvage were also collected	AAA
	December 22, 1914		Battalion at WURST FARM. — The weather remained fresh. 2nd Lieut. Shaw rejoined the expired portion of WURST FARM. Enemy shelling was not severe. At night however, heavy fire developed on the left and the Battalion was called upon to "stand to" during the greater part of the early morning.	AAA

WAR DIARY SHEET 11K
or
INTELLIGENCE SUMMARY

Place	Date	Hour	Summary of Events and Information	Remarks and references to Appendices
Battalion at WURST FARM.	December 23, 1917		The morning was uneventful, and in the afternoon the Battalion was relieved at WURST FARM by the 5/6th ROYAL SCOTS. The men entrained near WURST FARM and were conveyed to DAMBRE CAMP where accommodation was taken over in huts.	
Battalion at DAMBRE CAMP	December 24, 1917 AM		Turner. Acted during the greater part of the day and cleaned up. In the afternoon Company Parades (for issue of new clothing) Christmas parcels, containing considerable gifts subscribed by the friends of the Glasgow Chamber of Commerce and the forerunners of the "Glasgow News" were also issued	
Battalion at DAMBRE CAMP	December 25, 1917		A typical Christmas day – no pageants, weather conditions – no parades, snow fell fairly overnight and there was frequent falls throughout the day. The Battalion being in Corps Reserve nothing in the nature of Christmas festivities could be permitted but the men were allowed to spend the greater part of the day at leisure, and the Christmas gifts supplied by the Chamber of Commerce provided reasonable fare.	
Battalion at DAMBRE CAMP	December 26, 1917		The day was passed quietly, parades being carried out under Company arrangements.	

WAR DIARY
or
INTELLIGENCE SUMMARY.

Place	Date	Hour	Summary of Events and Information	Remarks and references to Appendices
Dec 26 contd.			Preparations were commenced for the carrying out of the Divisional Relief which were to be effected on the 29/30th.	
	December 27, 1917.		Battalion at DAMBRE CAMP. - Conditions on the front were comparatively quiet during the day, but towards nightfall heavy artillery fire developed and word was received that the Battalion was to stand-to. We were not called upon to proceed up the line however, and after a while the firing quieted down.	
	December 28, 1917		Battalion at DAMBRE CAMP. - On the uneventful day unexcelled, continues on the front remaining quiet. The weather still continued cold, and snow lay heavily on the ground.	
	December 29, 1917		Battalion at DAMBRE CAMP. - Final arrangements were made for the relief, the transport leaving by road for the RECOUES AREA. The rest of the Battalion was detailed to proceed by train the following day. At night-time again heavy fire on the front and the putting up of the S.O.S. by the Division in the line resulted in the Battalion being told to stand-to but as on the previous occasion things resumed the normal after a while.	

Army Form C. 2118.

WAR DIARY SHEET 16
or
INTELLIGENCE SUMMARY.
(Erase heading not required)

Instructions regarding War Diaries and Intelligence Summaries are contained in F.S. Regs., Part II. and the Staff Manual respectively. Title pages will be prepared in manuscript.

Place	Date	Hour	Summary of Events and Information	Remarks and references to Appendices
	December 30, 1917		Battalion at DAMBRE CAMP. — The Battalion paraded about 10 P.M. and marched to ELVERDINGHE Station where they entrained. Towards night the men entrained at AUDRUICQ and set out by Route for the villages of LANDRETHUN and YEUSE. The march was through the snow and over ice-bound roads but was sternly arduous but it was ultimately accomplished and the men were enabled to spend a night rest in comfortable billets.	1394
	December 31, 1917		Battalion at LANDRETHUN & YEUSE. — "A" "B" and "C" Companies along with HEADQUARTERS were billeted in the former village, "D" Company being relegated to the latter place. The last day of a year which had probably been the hardest and most eventful in the history of the Battalion was passed amidst the peaceful surroundings of these villages, untouched by war. The beginning of the year had seen the Battalion in the line in the SERRE sector then had followed the battle days of BEAUMONT HAMEL, ROUVROY, the Battle of SAVY and the taking of FAYET, in the ST. QUENTIN area, a long period of rest at CAMIZY and thence by train and route into BELGIUM, being just en route to draw in at the battle of	

WAR DIARY SHEET 17.
or
INTELLIGENCE SUMMARY.

Army Form C. 2118.

Place	Date	Hour	Summary of Events and Information	Remarks and references to Appendices
	December 3, 1917 contd.		@ MESSINES. Three board months were spent in the line in the NIEUPORT sector, and the ST GEORGES sector, and then, after a short spell before the Battalion went (forward) to PASSCHENDAELE.	AHM
			END.	

W.H. Manton, MAJOR,
COMMANDING 17th (S) Battalion, H.L.I.

WAR DIARY

FROM JANUARY 1, 1918.
TO JANUARY 31, 1918.

VOLUME 12.

[signature] MAJOR,
COMMANDING, 17th (S) BATTN H.L.I.

Army Form C. 2118.

Sheet 1.

WAR DIARY
or
INTELLIGENCE SUMMARY.
(Erase heading not required.)

Instructions regarding War Diaries and Intelligence Summaries are contained in F. S. Regs., Part II. and the Staff Manual respectively. Title pages will be prepared in manuscript.

Place	Date	Hour	Summary of Events and Information	Remarks and references to Appendices
	January 1st, 1918.		Battalion at LANDRETHUN and YEUSE :- The first day of the New Year was passed quietly on the rest areas. The fields in the surroundings were thickly laden with snow, this rendering the possibility of outdoor training somewhat remote. A Commanding Officer's Parade was taken by Major W W Thorton on a football ground opposite "A" Company billets, and for the rest of the day the men were at liberty.	☐
	January 2nd, 1918.		Battalion at LANDRETHUN and YEUSE :- Routine was continued on somewhat similar lines, the guard being taken daily by the R.S.M. for drill purposes, no mounting. The issue of leave for the Brigade was considerably increased. It was arranged to celebrate the New Year on the 3rd inst., this day to be observed as a general holiday.	☐
	January 3rd, 1918.		Battalion at LANDRETHUN and YEUSE :- With the exception of making preparations for the New Year feast in evening, Companies were allowed to rest during the whole of the day. In spite of provisioning difficulties, ample arrangements had been made for providing the men enjoying a seasonable repast in the evening. Companies sat down to a feast of roast pork - notice only a few hours however had been had- pig. There was soup, haggis, plum pudding, apple dumpling, cake and cigarettes etcetera ad-lib of beer being also provided. The Commanding	☐

Sheet 2

WAR DIARY
INTELLIGENCE SUMMARY

Army Form C. 2118.

Instructions regarding War Diaries and Intelligence Summaries are contained in F. S. Regs., Part II. and the Staff Manual respectively. Title pages will be prepared in manuscript.

(Erase heading not required.)

Place	Date	Hour	Summary of Events and Information	Remarks and references to Appendices
January,	3rd,	1918	Continued. Officer accompanied by Major G. R. S. Paterson, M.C., and the Adjutant visited each company in turn to wish them the compliments of the season, and the evening finished with song and story.	A
January,	4th	1918	Battalion at LANDRETHUN and YEUSE :- Work was resumed again in earnest as far as the weather conditions would permit. Parades in the forenoon completed the working parts of the day, arrangements being in progress for a more extensive programme of training.	A
January,	5th,	1918	Battalion at LANDRETHUN and YEUSE :- The day was uneventful, training being pursued quietly as far as weather and the condition of the ground would permit. In the evening Lieut.-Col. J. Inglis rejoined the Battalion from course and resumed command.	A
January,	6th,	1918	Battalion at LANDRETHUN and YEUSE :- The day being Sunday Church Parades were held in the Church LANDRETHUN and elsewhere. These were followed by an inspection of companies by the Commanding Officer. Intimation was received in the evening that the Corps Commander would inspect the Brigade Group on Tuesday, 9th inst.	A
January,	7th,	1918.	Battalion at LANDRETHUN and YEUSE :- The inclemency of the weather did not permit of out-door training. Word was received that the Battalion would move to the forward area for work on the 11th inst. Instructions were issued for the transport to proceed on 8th inst. by stages	A

Sheet 3

WAR DIARY

Army Form C. 2118.

INTELLIGENCE SUMMARY.

(Erase heading not required.)

Instructions regarding War Diaries and Intelligence Summaries are contained in F. S. Regs., Part II. and the Staff Manual respectively. Title pages will be prepared in manuscript.

Place	Date	Hour	Summary of Events and Information	Remarks and references to Appendices
January,	7th 1918		Continued to MURAT CAMP near YPRES. Arrangements were made to move the Battalion by bus on the 9th inst.	A
January,	8th 1918		Battalion at LANDRETHUN & YEUSE :- The Corps Commandant Inspector being cancelled for the Battalion and weather continuing training had to be carried on indoors. Full arrangements were made for move on the following day.	A
January,	9th 1918		The Battalion moved off in the morning and was picked up by bus and after a cold journey in a heavy snow storm arrived at MURAT CAMP late at night. The Battalion then came under the Command of the 35th Division.	A
January,	10th 1918		Battalion at MURAT CAMP :- The camp was in a very bad condition and the day was spent in cleaning up and improving the camp. Details of working parties required for the following day were received and arrangements made.	A
January,	11th 1918		Battalion at MURAT CAMP :- Working parties comprising 270 men were sent for work under C.R.E. 35th Division and all work was satisfactorily carried out.	A
January,	12th 1918		Battalion at MURAT CAMP :- Working parties were supplied as on previous day.	A

Sheet 1X

WAR DIARY

INTELLIGENCE SUMMARY.

(Erase heading not required.)

Army Form C. 2118.

Place	Date	Hour	Summary of Events and Information	Remarks and references to Appendices
January	13th 1918		Battalion at MURAT CAMP :- Working parties as for previous day were supplied	B
January	14th 1918		Battalion at MURAT CAMP :- Working parties as for previous day were supplied	B
January	15th 1918		Battalion at MURAT CAMP :- A violent storm raged all night and many of the tents were blown down causing great trouble to the men. The usual work parties supplied were mostly returned, as work was impossible, owing to the weather conditions. The storm abated towards mid-day and at was then possible to start restoring the camp to a habitable condition.	B
January	16th 1918		Battalion at MURAT CAMP :- Working parties were supplied as on previous day. Major W.W. Morton assumed command of the Battalion during the absence of Lieut. Col. J. Inglis on leave.	B
January	17th 1918		Battalion at MURAT CAMP :- Working parties were supplied as on previous day.	B
January	18th 1918		Battalion at MURAT CAMP :- The whole Battalion was employed on draining the Camp lines. Major G.R.S. Paterson, M.O. assumed command of the Battalion during the absence of Major W.W. Morton in Hospital.	B

Army Form C. 2118.

Sheet 5

WAR DIARY
INTELLIGENCE SUMMARY.
(Erase heading not required.)

Instructions regarding War Diaries and Intelligence Summaries are contained in F. S. Regs., Part II. and the Staff Manual respectively. Title pages will be prepared in manuscript.

Place	Date	Hour	Summary of Events and Information	Remarks and references to Appendices
January,	19th 1918		Battalion at MURAT CAMP :- The usual working parties were supplied for work on the Army lines. Owing to the improvements on the weather various improvements were made in the camp.	AB
January,	20th 1918		Battalion at MURAT CAMP :- To-day witnessed the advent of the "Battalion Intelligence News Sheet", inaugurated to keep all ranks fully informed of the principal events of the day, as regards the war. The usual working parties were supplied.	AB
January,	21st 1918		Battalion at MURAT CAMP :- The usual work parties were supplied. Casualties amounted to 1 o.r. wounded.	AB
January,	22nd 1918		Battalion at MURAT CAMP :- The usual work parties were supplied. Battalion came under Command of 97th Infantry Brigade from attachment with 55th Division.	AB
January,	23rd 1918		Battalion at MURAT CAMP :- The Battalion spent the day cleaning up. The Commanding Officer inspected camp in the afternoon.	AB
January,	24th 1918		Battalion at MURAT CAMP :- The Commanding Officer provided a cinema entertainment for the Battalion at ELVERDINGHE which was greatly appreciated	AB

Sheet 6

WAR DIARY
INTELLIGENCE SUMMARY
(Erase heading not required)

Army Form C. 2118.

Place	Date	Hour	Summary of Events and Information	Remarks and references to Appendices
January	25th 1918		The Battalion left MURAT CAMP at 12 noon for a camp near WOESTON. On arrival the Battalion came under command of the 1st Division.	B
January	26th 1918		Battalion at VAN DAMME :- Work parties consisted of 'C' & 'D' Companies & H.Q. were supplied for work under 1st Division R.E.	B
January	27th 1918		Battalion at VAN DAMME :- Preparations were completed for relief of 10th Gloucester in Reserve in the HET SAS Sector and by 3 pm the relief had been successfully accomplished. Battalion H.Q. was established at BOCHE CROSS ROADS	B
January	28th 1918		Battalion in Reserve of HET SAS SECTOR :- Companies worked on improvements of accommodation, and at night all companies provided carrying parties to Right and Left Battalions in the line. Situation very quiet.	
January	29th 1918		Battalion in Reserve of HET SAS SECTOR :- Companies worked on improvements of accommodation, and at night all companies provided carrying parties to Right and Left Battalions in the line. Situation very quiet.	
January	30th 1918		Battalion in Reserve of HET SAS SECTOR :- Companies worked on billet improvements and provided carrying parties at night as on previous day.	

Army Form C. 2118.

Shiet 7
WAR DIARY
or
INTELLIGENCE SUMMARY.
(Erase heading not required.)

Place	Date	Hour	Summary of Events and Information	Remarks and references to Appendices
	January 30	1918	Continued. Situation normal. Our guns were active also aircraft. Little enemy retaliation.	FD/
	January 31	1918	Battalion in Reserve of HET SAS SECTOR :- Battalion work on improvement of billets. The Commanding Officer was informed by the Brigadier to-day that the reorganisation of the Army necessitated the disbanding of the Battalion.	FD/

Chs Cakew, MAJOR,
COMMANDING, 17TH (S)/BATTN. H.L.I.